Did You Choose Your Parents?

A Secret Service Agent's Quest to Break the Presidential Curse

To our good neighbor, Linda Woods

Jan Marie

**JAN MARIE &
BOB RITTER**

Bob Ritter

CALVERT PRESS
9440 Old Solomons Island RD #445
Owings, MD 20736
calvertpress@yahoo.com

Manufactured in the United States of America

ISBN 978-0-9888502-2-4

www.secretservicebook.com

DEDICATION

This work is dedicated to those among us who are here to advance the consciousness of man.

"I see things most people don't."

Bob Ritter

CHAPTERS

FOREWORD

This is the true story of a young man's hopes and dreams, his goals and aspirations. I had the honor of working with Bob when I was the Special Agent in Charge of the U.S. Secret Service Washington Field Office. Worthy of trust and confidence, Bob exemplified the best traditions of the Secret Service: courage, duty, honesty, justice, and loyalty. He chose the Secret Service not for fame or fortune, but for patriotic ideals and civic service. The sacrifices he made for his country adversely affected his family and personal life. For the Secret Service, it was a time of too many responsibilities for too few resources.

Our nation owes a great deal of thanks to federal agents like Bob Ritter as well as the loved ones who stand by them. Like those brave Americans who serve in our armed forces, our nation's federal law enforcement officers deserve our highest respect and gratitude. Their dedication and sense of duty come at a heavy personal cost, and we are all the beneficiaries of this selflessness.

Gerald W. Bechtle

Gerald W. Bechtle

Deputy Director, United States Secret Service (Retired)

AUTHOR'S NOTE

D id You Choose Your Parents? is the fact-based account of the journey my husband (Bob Ritter) and I traveled through life, especially during the Secret Service years. While writing our memoir: I gained additional insight into some of our most intimate recollections. The reasoning behind the road Bob chose and other important life decisions became clear and understandable.

Bob has held a life-long inhibition to revealing these most private and provocative details. Fearful that these beliefs would not be believed and subject him to ridicule, he has only divulged this information to immediate family members, until now.

With the advent of the Internet and social media, some have described somewhat similar memories. With others stepping forward and in the troubling times our world is in, Bob now believes that these disclosures will be *beneficial* to mankind. Hopefully, it will inspire others to reveal their accounts and to foster fellowship among the peoples of the world.

The narrative offered in *Did You Choose Your Parents?* weaves interesting American history into an exciting true-crime memoir. Strategies for detecting dangerousness in individuals and the need to reduce the culture of violence will be passed on to readers.

I can assure you that our book is factual, honest, and truthful to the best of our knowledge and memory. I have full confidence that Bob *truly* believes what he has revealed to me, and I believe Bob without a doubt. ...

Jan Marie Ritter

Did You Choose Your Parents?

Chapter 1

3-30-81

I'll *never* forget when I heard the news. It was mid-afternoon Monday, March 30, 1981. An overcast sky with drizzle enveloped the Washington, D.C. area in a lining of gray. My class of fourth and fifth graders was reading silently at their desks. Setting an example, I was reading too. My thoughts drifted between the remaining school day and the coming evening with my family. Only an occasional cough or shuffling of feet interrupted the calm. It had been a productive and quiet start to the week—as quiet as a suburban Maryland elementary school could be—*maybe too quiet.*

Suddenly, the classroom door swung open with an alarming creak, snapping me back to the present. In darted Principal Jo Fisher; she headed straight for my desk. It wasn't unusual for Jo to visit classes, but this time her face expressed worry and concern—in an intensity I hadn't seen before. Reaching my side, she leaned down close to my ear and softly asked, "Jan, is Bob working today?"

The unusualness of the question along with her troubled look made me immediately apprehensive. My husband, Bob Ritter, was a special agent with the United States Secret Service (USSS). He had been in federal law enforcement for about nine years and was currently stationed in Washington at the Secret Service's Intelligence Division (ID).

Fearing what Jo might say next, I almost didn't want to answer. Holding back some anxiety, I summoned enough nerve to reply, "Yes, Bob works just about every day." In an instant, Jo's face turned pale with distress; her head slumped toward the floor. The textbook dropped from my hands, landing on the desk with a clunk. "What's wrong, Jo?" I uttered.

Jo took a deep breath as she raised her head. Her eyes met mine, and she quickly turned her head to the side—trying to shield me from the increased concern her face displayed. Jo's next words fell from her lips straight to my heart. "There's been a shooting involving the president, and some people have been injured. Go to the media center. I'll watch your class."

A sense of dread seized me as I ran—heart pounding furiously—all the way to the school's media center. Inside, I found some of our support personnel crowded around the television set—with eyes fixed to the screen. News was breaking of an assassination attempt on President Ronald Reagan—at the Washington Hilton Hotel.

At first, the news coverage was spotty and left much to the imagination. Later that afternoon, video taken during the incident appeared on the networks. Terror overtook me like a speeding bullet. This wasn't a Hollywood thriller; this was all too real. President Reagan was coming out of the hotel toward his limousine, smiling and waving to the crowd. Without warning, gunshots rang out; pandemonium ensued. Some people near the president were hit. My heart fluttered; one was a Secret Service agent. During the first quick take, this agent resembled Bob in general features. My worst nightmare was upon me. Thankfully, it appeared that the president was unharmed.

Even though I knew Bob had most likely *not* been assigned to the Washington Hilton that day, I held my breath until the video segment was re-played, and I was positive the agent wounded was neither Bob nor anyone I recognized. Although sad for those injured, I involuntarily gasped with relief. My display of thankfulness was noticeable and understandable to those in the room. They were aware of my husband's occupation, and several hugged me with compassion for my emotions.

I was grateful I hadn't seen Bob in the video. Only 69 days before, he had worked the *same* arrival/departure area. Bob had been the Secret Service Intelligence Division advance agent for the presidential inaugural ball held at the Washington Hilton.

Bob considered it the *most dangerous* site in D.C. for the president; therefore, he had specifically asked for the assignment. He wanted to ensure that an agent fully aware of the security vulnerabilities at that location would be handling the protective intelligence duties. Bob had been worried about the protective survey changes the USSS had made at the Washington Hilton during his tenure at the Washington Field Office (WFO). Bob's *unheeded* warnings had been prophetic.

As the TV was switched between channels that afternoon, all networks were initially reporting that the president had *not* been injured. This raised our spirits. Later, more horror unfolded, as the networks corrected earlier bulletins regarding the president. The president *had* been injured and was undergoing emergency treatment at George Washington University Hospital. In addition, it was reported that a Secret Service agent, a Metropolitan Police officer, and White House Press Secretary James Brady had also been wounded.

School dismissal brought a surge of classroom teachers to the media center, as word of the assassination attempt spread. Everyone wanted to learn the latest news. Some asked me if Bob was involved in the incident. I told them it was my belief that he was working at Secret Service Headquarters as an Intelligence Division duty agent. All were very concerned, and I was appreciative of the support and comfort they gave.

The replaying of the video became overwhelming—particularly the chilling sight of Mr. Brady's motionless head lying in a pool of his own blood. I had to turn away and couldn't watch any longer.

Leaving the media center, I went to look for Jo. I wanted to thank her for her kindness and concern. She was now holding down the school's office, while intently following the news via radio. When Jo saw me, she turned down the volume and searched my face—looking for telltale signs regarding Bob. I related that I hadn't seen Bob in any of the news footage. It was my belief that he hadn't been at the Hilton. She was relieved to hear that bit of good news. We sadly discussed the turnaround of reports regarding the president. We were devastated that he had been shot.

Attempting to get my mind off the tragedy, I told Jo I was going back to my classroom to work on lesson plans. She replied sharply: "No, you should go home *now*. Carrie and Robbie will need you to sort this out." Of course, she was right. My 11-year-old daughter and 6-year-old son would need answers to their questions and easing of any fears caused by the tragic news. This was *not* a normal day.

I hurried to my car and drove to my son's after school caregiver while thinking of how best to handle the situation. Fortunately, Robbie was not aware of the shooting. The caregiver, a friend and neighbor, had purposely shielded Robbie from the news. I would do likewise until both of my children were together.

Once home, I kept Robbie to his normal routine. Bursting through the front door, Carrie arrived later that afternoon. She ran to me with outstretched arms and a puzzled look. While we were still embraced, she said in an uncertain tone: "Mommy, something about Daddy's work was on TV. The teachers told us about it."

"I know, honey," I replied.

Carrie and I got Robbie, and we went to the family room and settled down on the floor in front of the television set. I told them as calmly as I could: "A terrible thing happened today. A bad man has shot our president along with some other people. Dad's okay, but a Secret Serviceman, just like Dad, was one of the people hurt."

I turned on the television, and we watched the news coverage and videotape of the attempt. I explained what they were seeing. Afterwards, both Robbie and Carrie looked at me with astonishment, and Carrie exclaimed: "That's what Daddy does! It's not fair that he would have to be shot for the president."

It suddenly occurred to me that my children didn't really understand what their father did for a living. They had only seen

Bob in the work setting of White House tours, Christmas parties, Easter egg hunts, and other fun activities.

Hugging my children tightly to comfort them, I said: "Yes, Secret Service men and women work hard to keep the president safe. It can sometimes be dangerous—like today, but good people have to stand up to bad people. Your dad knows what he's doing, and we don't need to worry about him. He'll be okay."

I turned the TV off, so Robbie and Carrie wouldn't become permeated with the graphic images of real-life violence. They went to their rooms for homework and reading, while I headed to the kitchen to prepare dinner.

I knew there was no need to set a place for Bob. Although he was working the 7:00 a.m. to 3:00 p.m. shift, the attempt on the president's life would necessitate him being held over. The best I could hope for would be a telephone call from Bob, letting me know his situation. It would be reassuring to hear his voice.

While making dinner, I listened to the radio to stay abreast of the president's surgery and the condition of the others injured. The roller coaster ride of emotion continued. It had been announced that James Brady had died. Deeply saddened by the news, I rejoiced when Mr. Brady's death was retracted. Reports now listed him as alive but unfortunately gravely wounded.

The Secret Service agent wounded was identified as Tim McCarthy. I remembered the name as an agent Bob had shared hotel rooms with—during an overseas trip of Secretary of State Henry Kissinger. Bob had mentioned that he and Tim were members of the same college social fraternity—at different universities. I felt sorry for Tim's family and wondered if he was married.

Every time the phone rang, I dropped what I was doing (in hope it was Bob) and ran to grab the receiver. Each time, it was a family member or friend inquiring about Bob and the assassination attempt. I briefly told them what I knew and that I appreciated their concern. I apologized for having to keep the calls short; I needed to leave the phone free—for whenever Bob could call.

Later that evening, Bob did telephone; it was a great relief to hear from him and to confirm his safety. His calm and confident voice was quite a contrast to the confusion and uncertainty of the television and radio coverage. Since the attempt on President Reagan's life, Bob had worked nonstop at the ID duty desk. He had no idea when he would be able to come home. Bob told me he loved me and missed me. He asked me to give the kids his love and to kiss them goodnight for him.

I remarked how unbelievable it was that the assassination attempt had taken place at the Washington Hilton—the very site that Bob had been worried about. His reply: "It was a dangerous spot. Honey, I have to go now. See you when I get home. Love you."

I immediately told Robbie and Carrie of Bob's call. As I put them to bed, we said a prayer for Bob, President Reagan, Mr. Brady, Agent McCarthy, and the injured Metropolitan Police officer, who was identified as Thomas Delahanty. I kissed the kids goodnight and sent along Bob's love.

Restlessly and anxiously waiting for Bob to arrive, I passed the remainder of the evening on the living room sofa. Several times, I arose to my feet when I heard a car approaching—only to be considerably disappointed when it didn't stop. Finally, I heard Bob's car pulling into our driveway. I met him at the door with a kiss and an embrace.

Bob was exhausted. The collar to his wrinkled dress shirt was unbuttoned; his tie hung out of the breast pocket of his suit jacket. He was slumped over and moved slowly. Bob had gotten up at 4:30 a.m. in order to arrive at Secret Service Headquarters for the 6:45 a.m. relief of the midnight shift.

"Do you want something to eat?" I asked.

In a hoarse voice, Bob answered: "No thanks, I'll wait till breakfast. I just want to get some sleep."

"What time do you have to go in tomorrow?"

"Regular time," he replied.

We went to our bedroom where I helped Bob off with his clothes. After collapsing onto the bed and closing his eyes, he found enough energy to say: "It was close. We almost lost the president today. It looks like everyone is going to be okay—except Secretary Brady. He's in a bad way. It shouldn't have happened. I wish I could have been there. It shouldn't have happened."

I had many questions, but mercifully I let Bob rest. In spite of his long day, the Secret Service was still requiring him to be back at 6:45 a.m. I set his alarm and snuggled with Bob in bed. It was good to have him safely home and close to me. I gave him a goodnight kiss and told him I loved him. Bob didn't respond; he was already asleep.

The day had taken on a *surreal* dimension. Bob's worst fears had been realized. Sadly, he had been proven right. The President of the United States was *nearly* assassinated and three others seriously injured.

What follows is the true story of my husband's efforts to prevent this tragedy. Bob's dedication to this personal life mission was extraordinary.

You're invited to come along as we relive this quest. There'll be fun and adventure—along with some sorrow and disappointment. Hopefully, you'll also experience some moments that will resonate in *your* life's story.

Chapter 2

The Presidential Curse

I was always intrigued by Bob's dedication to breaking the Presidential Curse. Also known as Tecumseh's Curse, the 20-Year Curse, and the Zero Year Curse, it has supposedly cost the lives of seven U.S. Presidents.

In 1808, Shawnee Chief Tecumseh and his brother, The Prophet, founded an Indian settlement at Tippecanoe in the Indiana Territory. Tecumseh wanted to unite the Indian people to fight the westward expansion of white settlers. Tippecanoe was the capital of their tribal confederation.

In 1811, Tecumseh was in the South recruiting warriors when the governor of the territory, William Henry Harrison, decided to act. He raised an army and marched to Tippecanoe with the intent of settling the matter by treaty or force. Harrison's men camped outside the Indian village upon word from The Prophet that he wished a meeting. Tecumseh had warned his brother not to engage the white man until the Indian alliance could be strengthened.

In spite of Tecumseh's warning, his brother led a surprise attack on Harrison's campsite the following morning. Casualties were heavy on both sides, and the Indians finally withdrew. The Prophet was disgraced, and he eventually fled to the Northwest Territory as the other tribes scattered. The next day, Harrison entered the deserted settlement and burned it to the ground.

Chief Tecumseh returned to find his capital in ashes and his dreams of an Indian nation shattered. Tecumseh then called on the gods to curse Governor Harrison and his people. The gods answered Tecumseh with prophecy. Harrison would one day become the Great White Chief, but he would die soon after.

Each Great White Chief chosen every 20 years after Harrison would also die in office. This would be punishment for the white nation and serve as a reminder of the sorrow of the Indian people.

Tecumseh and his followers would fight for the British in the War of 1812. Harrison was given command of the U.S. Army in the Northwest. Tecumseh was killed in battle in 1813 by troops led by General Harrison.

After the war, Harrison returned to public life in Ohio and served in the U.S. House of Representatives and the U.S. Senate. In 1840, he successfully ran for the presidency on the campaign slogan, 'Tippecanoe and Tyler, Too.' He gave a long inaugural address on a cold, blustery day, and it rained as he rode on horseback in his inaugural parade. Newly elected President Harrison caught a cold that turned into pneumonia. He died about a month later. Harrison was the *first* president to die in office. Tecumseh's Curse had begun.

The curse had fascinated Bob since childhood when his grandfather presented him a 1940s copy of Robert Ripley's *Believe it or Not!* The book featured an entry which stated: "United States presidents elected every twenty years since 1840 died in office." Below that were listed the six presidents with their election years: Harrison (1840), Lincoln (1860), Garfield (1880), McKinley (1900), Harding (1920), and Roosevelt (1940). Next came a blank line with several question marks for 1960. ...

That entry in Ripley's *Believe it or Not!* along with radio and television shows regarding Chief Tecumseh's Curse captivated Bob. In the late 1950s, Bob saw the movie *The Tall Target* on television. He was inspired by the film, and it further stirred his fascination with presidential assassination and its prevention.

Actor Dick Powell portrayed New York Police Detective *John Kennedy*, who dramatically prevented the assassination of President-elect Abraham Lincoln on his way to Washington for his 1861 inaugural. Kennedy became a hero to Bob along with Detective Allan Pinkerton who was actually the operative in real

life. The real *John Kennedy* was the New York city superinten-
dent of police and involved in the initial investigation of the suspected plot.

The curse was fulfilled once again when President *John Kennedy* was assassinated on November 22, 1963. Bob remembers
the day well. As his high school newspaper's photography edi-
tor, Bob was in the school's dark room doing some work when
the news broke on the radio. Bob immediately rushed to the
school's office to inform staff. Bob was struck by the fact that
the president elected in 1960 and subsequently assassinated
had the same name as one of his childhood heroes.

While students at the University of Maryland, Bob and I met
and started dating in 1967. At that time, Bob had planned either
to go into federal law-enforcement or to law school after gradu-
ation. The assassination of Martin Luther King, Jr. (MLK) and
Robert F. Kennedy (RFK) in 1968—along with our marriage—
weighed heavily on Bob. Bob dropped his law school ambition.
He decided to pursue a career in federal law-enforcement, eventually with the U.S. Secret Service.

The first time Bob informed me about the Presidential Curse
was on May, 15, 1972. Bob had undergone a morning operation,
so he could be medically-approved for the U.S. Park Police.
While he was recovering in his room that afternoon after the
procedure, news broke over the television networks of an assassination attempt on presidential candidate and former Alabama
Governor George Wallace. The attempt had taken place at a
shopping center in Laurel, Maryland, about 20 miles away.

We had been to the shopping center and were familiar with it.
Bob watched the video of the attempt and told me the answer
was "in the crowd." He expounded on Tecumseh's Curse and
told me the main reason he eventually wanted to join the Secret
Service was to prevent the assassination of the president who
would be elected in 1980. Bob felt he was up to the challenge
and had some ideas on making executive protection better.

"Let's hope we never have to go through another presidential assassination," Bob declared. "Yet we can learn from past mistakes. History doesn't have to repeat itself. We can break the Presidential Curse."

"So, all presidents elected every 20 years since 1840 have died before completing their terms?" I asked incredulously.

"That's right. Starting in 1840 with William Henry Harrison, the hero of Tippecanoe, every president—elected or reelected in a year ending in zero—died in office. Of those seven presidents, four were assassinated."

"That's unbelievable," I said. "It also says something about our society. But Bobbie, you don't believe in curses—do you?"

"No, but I do believe in patterns of history. Patterns that show a sitting president is going to die about every 20 years—mostly by assassination. These assassinations can be studied for the purpose of prediction and prevention. Socio-scientific analysis can be made. The results can suggest successful strategies. We can't change the past, but we can change our *tomorrows*."

"Well, if anyone can figure it out, you can," I said in admiration. I believed that Bob could accomplish most anything—once he set his mind to the task.

I took Bob's goal of preventing assassination as just something he was passionate about. Through the years, it would become a central theme and motivator of his career decisions. It would be decades later until Bob revealed the inner drive that had motivated him. ...

Chapter 3

Earliest Memories

Bob and I were traveling by car to South Jersey to visit his mom (Ruth Ritter) for the 2002 holiday season. It had been a couple of difficult years with his dad passing in 2000. That was followed by the death of Bob's sister in 2002. Bob had also been diagnosed and treated for cancer, which reminded us of our own mortality.

On the drive up, I thought I would use the time to query Bob regarding his past zeal for breaking the Presidential Curse on background for our book. During his Secret Service years, it seemed that he placed that goal above all else, including his family.

I kept probing and was caught off guard when Bob took on a somber tone and said, "Okay, I'm going to tell you something that I've *never* told anyone before. You deserve to know. Please don't think I'm crazy or losing my mind.

"I know I had at least one past life. ... And I agreed to certain things for this one."

I don't think I said anything for a moment or two. I had been married to Bob for over 30 years; I knew he wasn't kidding. He was as serious as I had ever seen him. Yet, to my knowledge, Bob had always championed scientific methodology and rationalism. To say I was shocked at what I had just heard would be an understatement!

I finally said, "I'm all ears."

"The earliest memories I can recall were before birth," Bob began. "I was connected to others solely by consciousness. Some

of them were the souls of past loved ones. We communi
thoughts.

"I was eventually questioned by a panel about some o
cisions I had made during my most recent life.

"Immediately after giving the reasoning for my actions, I was offered an opportunity for another animated life. Information about my suggested future parents was revealed. I was told they were of good heredity: My father's lineage descended from courageous knights and my mother from ancestors with exemplary ideals. Additional background about my future parents was given.

"I didn't have to accept the offer, but it seemed to me that it had been some time since my prior life, and I was wanting to get back in the game.

"There were some conditions. The *collective* consciousness or whatever you want to call it was horrified at the development of the atomic bomb and its use on Japanese civilian targets by the United States. The first atomic bomb was dropped over Hiroshima on August 6, 1945, exactly one year before my rebirth. The second A-bomb was dropped on Nagasaki three days later. It's estimated over 100,000 people perished due to the initial blasts with tens of thousands dying in the following weeks due to radiation poisoning. The collective feared the spreading of these weapons and their use in even more destructive and deadly wars on Earth.

"The collective would permit me to keep some of my higher consciousness with its special abilities. In return, I had to vow to dedicate my life to furthering world peace and similar goals. I was told I would know how best to do this and to *trust my inner voice at all times*. I would need to be persistent and to make personal sacrifices. I would see things that most don't. I was given guidance to stay the course and not to bow to popular convention or to use my special abilities for worldly pleasures over idealistic pursuits. I was warned to keep all of this to myself, for my own good.

"I was contemplating the offer when suddenly I heard, 'We need your decision, *now.*'

"I answered with a quick yes. *Instantaneously*, I found my consciousness in a hospital room where I was being born. Even though I had self-awareness that I was now that baby, it was like I was not fully in the body yet. I observed, heard, and understood everything that was happening in the room. My consciousness was hovering there and witnessing everything that was going on. That continued when I was transferred from the delivery suite to the nursery and eventually discharged with my mom.

"One early incident stands out. After sometime at home, my parents held a little gathering of family, friends, and neighbors. I still had the power of being able to comprehend everything that was being said around me but, of course, was unable to speak.

"I'm in my crib in one of the bedrooms, and I can hear everyone talking and laughing out in the living room. Suddenly, a couple enters the bedroom and come over to the crib. The man says to the lady, 'Did they have a boy or a girl?'

"'I don't know,'" she replies.

"He then quickly proceeds to unpin my diapers and after checking me blurts out, 'It's a boy.'

"Just then my mom hurries into the room and sternly demands to know what's going on. He cries out, 'Ruth, I was just checking to see what sex your baby was.' His lady companion stands there speechless and looking embarrassed.

"My mom says, 'Didn't you see the blue blanket? You could have asked. Please go to the living room. I'll take care of his diaper.' My mom was upset."

Bob took a short pause before affirming, "Jan, I truly believe what I just told you. It's not flashbacks or fantasy. I really experienced it as it happened."

A couple of moments passed, while I was thinking over all I had just heard. I eventually said, "Bobbie, this is all on too high a level for my understanding. I don't have any memories like that, and it's a lot to process. I do believe you, and it certainly explains some of the decisions you made in life and your dedication to the Secret Service."

"Tell you what," Bob stated. "I'll mention the story I just told you to my mom this weekend; we'll see if she can remember it."

Bob did relate the story to Ruth, and her face perked up in astonishment. "Yes, I do remember that. It was creepy! But how in the world did you know?" He also recited something of an intimate medical nature that the doctor had told her after the delivery. She confirmed every word.

It was a trip I'll *never* forget!

Chapter 4

School Years and Beyond

Bob was a precocious child. He whizzed through elementary school and junior high, scoring well in the classroom and on standardized tests. His school system actually suggested that Bob skip a grade, but his mom wouldn't agree. Bob's heightened cognitive skills were a great asset to his learning and achievement.

It was the same in high school. Bob graduated fifth in a class of over 400 students, while earning scholastic, athletic, and activity honors. Only one male finished higher. Bob was inducted into his high school hall of fame and even offered a career position as a professional photographer due to his ability.

When I met Bob at the University of Maryland, he had an excellent grade point average and was a respected campus leader. His activities earned him an induction into Omicron Delta Kappa National Leadership Honorary and a listing in Who's Who in American Colleges and Universities. Bob also impressed me with his intelligence, maturity, and self-assuredness. And *yes*, I thought him handsome and sexy.

The year 1968 was a major milestone in our lives. We fell deeply in love and married in spite of parental reservations that we wait until we both graduate.

With the assassination of MLK and RFK, Bob set a goal of becoming a Secret Service agent. He wanted to prevent the assassination of leaders who might lead us to better international relations, better domestic policies, and racial equality and harmony. The death and destruction by riots that ripped America after MLK's tragic murder was devastating to Bob as well as the "what ifs" had JFK, MLK, and RFK not been cut down in their prime.

Living with Bob, I saw firsthand how important his career goals had become. He probably could have become a Secret Service agent right after graduating college, but he wanted the knowledge and experience gained from working as a federal police officer. He also enjoyed helping people, and uniformed law enforcement gave him plenty of opportunities to do so.

Bob and I were similar in our desire to help people and to pursue rewarding careers. I had accepted a teaching position with the Prince George's County Maryland School System. I believed I was making a difference and helping to create a better society. We and many others of our generation had been inspired by the "New Frontier" of President John F. Kennedy. In his 1961 Inaugural address, JFK urged, "And so, my fellow Americans: Ask not what your country can do for you; ask what you can do for your country."

Like Bob, my profession was not something I got into by accident or convenience. I truly felt I was answering my country's call. Prince George's County was struggling with court-ordered desegregation. Amidst the turmoil of mandatory busing and integration, I chose Prince George's over other school systems with lesser challenges. Bob and I were committed to work for a better America.

Bob had many memorable incidents during his U.S. Park Police years, including a brush with an individual who would later attempt to assassinate President Richard Nixon.

It was in late 1973. The Watergate Affair dominated national headlines at the time. After President Nixon fired Watergate Special Prosecutor Archibald Cox, there were calls for the president's impeachment. Anti-Nixon demonstrations and protests sprung up in Washington, D.C. One demonstrator demanding Nixon's impeachment was a short, stocky, middle-aged man named Samuel J. Byck. He was an unemployed salesman from Philadelphia, Pennsylvania. Byck had been turned down for a

Small Business Administration loan. After the rejection, Byck became an outspoken critic of President Nixon, whom he accused of oppressing the poor.

Byck had been to Washington before with his one-man demonstration. On that occasion, Park Police had warned Byck that he needed a permit to demonstrate on the White House sidewalk. When Byck refused to get one, Park Police arrested him.

Now once again, Byck was back on the White House sidewalk and carrying a protest sign. Several carloads of Park Police officers pulled up along Pennsylvania Avenue in front of the White House in order to monitor the day's demonstrations. One of the officers recognized Byck and asked the sergeant if Byck had a permit.

"No, I don't see him on the list. Check him out. If he doesn't have a permit and refuses to stop, arrest him."

The officer approached Byck with Bob standing by as backup. When asked if he had a permit, Byck became agitated and said he didn't need one. He refused to leave. The officer grabbed Byck's left arm and placed him under arrest. Byck resisted the officer's grasp, and Bob moved in to control Byck's right arm. Byck was whisked to the USPP patrol wagon where he was transported to D.C.'s Central Cell Block.

Unknown to Park Police, Byck had come to the attention of the U.S. Secret Service in 1972 for allegedly remarking that someone should kill President Nixon. Byck was interviewed by agents from the Philadelphia Field Office of the Secret Service. He became the subject of periodic Secret Service investigations. Unfortunately, Byck's mental state deteriorated.

On the morning of February 22, 1974 (Washington's Birthday), Samuel Byck drove to Baltimore/Washington International Airport (BWI) in Anne Arundel County, Maryland. Armed with a stolen .22-caliber handgun and a homemade gasoline bomb, Byck shot and killed an airport policeman who was screening passengers at a security checkpoint. Byck then stormed his way aboard a nearby Delta Airlines DC-9 jetliner.

Entering the cockpit through its unlocked door, Byck found the pilot and copilot readying the aircraft for a flight to Atlanta. Byck ordered the pilot to take off immediately. The pilot cautioned that he couldn't take off with the door of the plane still opened. Byck fired a warning shot into the cockpit. Two flight attendants ran off the plane, closing the main door behind them.

Byck again ordered the pilot to get the plane off the ground. The pilot answered that the wheels were still chocked and that the plane had not been cleared for departure. Upset, Byck fired another shot. Then, he grabbed a female passenger from the cabin and forced her into the cockpit to help fly the plane. Angered that the aircraft was not moving, Byck shot the pilot and copilot and returned the passenger to her seat. Byck grabbed another female passenger and dragged her into the cockpit. Again, Byck fired at the pilot and copilot.

Through the porthole of the door to the aircraft, a responding county police officer saw Byck moving between the cabin and the cockpit. The officer fired several times at the hijacker with his .38-caliber issued service revolver but couldn't penetrate the door's plexiglass window. Then, the officer fired the .357 Magnum revolver he had removed from the fallen airport policeman. Byck was hit twice. With the copilot fatally shot and the pilot severely wounded, Byck retreated into the cockpit where he committed suicide.

At the time, Byck's motives were not known. The incident looked like just another aircraft hijacking attempt. Subsequently, an audio tape was found in Byck's car. Byck had also mailed a tape recording to newspaper columnist Jack Anderson and others. On the tapes, Byck tells of "Operation Pandora's Box." Byck chillingly details his plan to hijack an airliner and to force the crew to fly it over downtown Washington, D.C. There, Byck would shoot the pilots and drive the control stick of the aircraft down toward the White House, causing the airliner to crash into the Executive Mansion. Byck's failed hijacking was in actuality an assassination attempt on President Richard Nixon.

Bob suspected that an incident that occurred only five days before might have influenced Byck. "It's the copycat phenomenon," Bob informed. "In some impressionable minds, certain incidents can inspire similar behavior. People who are unhappy with their lives, blame others for their problems, and are suicidal are especially susceptible. They see the notoriety gained by perpetrating an infamous act. The copycat sees a way to become famous and to gain some revenge. At the state their mind is in, it seems to be the only way they can get even and get some self-satisfaction. I've got to believe that the White House helicopter intrusion affected Byck."

In the early morning hours of Sunday, February 17, 1974, Private First Class (PFC) Robert K. Preston stole an Army UH-1B "Huey" helicopter from Fort Meade, Maryland—about 25 miles east of Washington, D.C. The 20-year-old Preston had washed out of the Army's flight school and was sent to Ft. Meade to become a helicopter mechanic.

Preston flew the stolen helicopter to the restricted airspace of the White House complex. There, he flew over the White House and hovered above the South Grounds. Unaware of the origins and intentions of the helicopter, Executive Protective Service (EPS) officers took no action.

The Huey left the area but returned later with a Maryland State Police (MSP) helicopter in pursuit. MSP had been notified that a rogue helicopter was flying erratically in the vicinity of BWI Airport. The MSP helicopter intercepted the rogue helicopter, following it down the Baltimore-Washington Parkway toward D.C. Once again, the Huey violated restricted airspace and approached the south side of the White House near the West Wing. This time, EPS officers opened up with pistols and shotguns. The rogue helicopter landed on the White House lawn and Preston was arrested.

Preston was eventually turned over to Army authorities. He was sentenced to a year at hard labor and fined $2,400. Although the President and Mrs. Nixon were not in Washington during the incident, matters of White House security had been raised. The incident received extensive media coverage. The pilot of the MSP helicopter indicated that Preston could have flown the stolen chopper into the White House at top speed (over 100 miles per hour). The MSP trooper believed that those on the ground would have been unable to prevent it. Did the Preston incident spawn Byck's plan for an aerial assault of the White House?

Bob had several close calls during his Park Police service. On one occasion, his cruiser was struck from behind while stopped along the George Washington Memorial Parkway near Arlington, Virginia. An inattentive motorist rear-ended Bob at about 40 miles per hour. It was one of those things a police spouse fears most. Bob's cruiser was on the northbound side of the parkway. The impact of the accident propelled the cruiser into the air where it turned around a complete 180 degrees before landing some feet from where it had been.

Miraculously, Bob only received whiplash, back injuries, and some bruises. The Park Police official who conducted the accident investigation remarked that Bob was very fortunate. The investigator stated it was a wonder the gas tank hadn't exploded from the impact. Also, if the cruiser had been propelled in the other direction, the car would have gone over a steep, high cliff that bordered that section of the parkway. Rocks and the Potomac River lay far below. It was certain that Bob would not have survived.

The back spasms and pain persisted; the doctor at the D.C. Police and Fire Clinic wanted to write Bob up for disability retirement. The doctor believed a law enforcement career would continue to aggravate these injuries, and Bob would be a liability to himself and others.

I *urged* Bob to take the disability retirement. The provisions of the retirement would have provided us financial stability, while permitting Bob to go to law school and to pursue a less rigorous career. Accepting the retirement, Bob would only be prohibited from serving as a law enforcement officer.

Bob steadfastly refused the offer, much to my dismay. It seemed to me that he certainly deserved the disability retirement and that he was making a huge mistake. It wasn't until Bob's 2002 disclosures that I understood the full reasoning behind Bob's rejection of the offer.

Chapter 5

SY

Having reached his two and a half-year anniversary with Park Police, Bob applied for an agent position with the U.S. Secret Service. As it turned out, Bob was told that the Secret Service had no immediate openings in its Washington Field Office. That fact along with an offer from the U.S. Department of State would cause Bob to take a detour on the road to his professional hopes and dreams.

While waiting for the Secret Service to open up, Bob served as a State Department Office of Security (SY) investigator and protection agent. During this time, the Secret Service protected Secretary of State Dr. Henry Kissinger, while SY protected Mrs. Kissinger.

Of the foreign trips Bob worked at State, one of the most memorable was the October 1974 visit of Secretary of State and Mrs. Kissinger to the former Soviet Union. At the time, Russia and the United States were still very much engaged in the Cold War. Soviet security forces harassed the USSS and SY advance teams on a number of occasions.

The intrigue began for Bob when he first arrived in Moscow and attempted to pass through immigration and customs. The Soviet official carefully inspected Bob's U.S. Diplomatic Passport. Then, the officer checked Bob's passport with a list of Americans arriving to advance Secretary of State Henry Kissinger's forthcoming visit. A moment later, the immigration officer looked up at Bob and barked, "Your name is not on the list." Handing Bob's passport back, the official firmly stated, "You are not permitted to enter the Soviet Union."

Bob protested, "I have a diplomatic passport with valid visa issued by your embassy in Washington."

The officer called to a supervisor, who was standing nearby. "Is there a problem?" asked the supervisor in accented English.

"He is not on the official list for the Kissinger delegation," replied the immigration officer.

The supervisor looked sternly at Bob: "Come with me. There will have to be an inquiry."

An SY agent in line behind Bob promised to send assistance after that agent cleared immigration and customs. The party was being met by the State Department assistant regional security officer (RSO). He would be sent to help Bob.

The supervisor escorted Bob to the immigration office. There, the official—with Bob's passport in one hand and a master list in the other—made his own check. Waving the list in front of Bob, the officer taunted: "This is very serious. You are not on the official list agreed between your country and the Ministry of Foreign Affairs."

"Let me see the list," Bob said in an assertive tone. The officer reluctantly handed the document to Bob. Perusing the list, a name caught Bob's eyes in the Js. "Look here," Bob stated emphatically as he pointed to the name. "There's a Robert *Jitter* listed. And that probably says security. It's a typing error. It's supposed to be me, Robert Ritter."

The official snatched the list back from Bob and took a quick look. Then to Bob's astonishment, the official remarked, "No, that's Robert *Jitter*."

"We don't have a Robert Jitter. There is no *Robert Jitter*! Someone made a mistake."

The officer sat down at his desk and began to dial the telephone. "I will have to consult the Ministry of Foreign Affairs." For about 10 minutes, the immigration supervisor navigated his way through a series of telephone conversations. As the official spoke in Russian, Bob had no idea how things were going.

In the meantime, the assistant RSO arrived at the office. Bob recapped the situation. The assistant RSO immediately turned to the immigration official and stated in a resolute voice: "I am from the U.S. Embassy. Why is this American diplomat being detained?"

The supervisor answered: "He is not on the official entry list. I am now awaiting a call from the Ministry of Foreign Affairs to determine his fate."

The assistant RSO spoke with increasing firmness: "I am familiar with the list submitted to the Soviet Embassy in Washington. Mr. Ritter was on that list and was issued an entry visa for this trip. Mr. Ritter needs to be cleared immediately. He is an *official* guest of your country."

The immigration supervisor replied in a conciliatory tone: "Please sit down. The ministry will be calling back soon."

"Mr. Ritter has proper credentials. This is becoming more than an inconvenience. You need to clear him now or a protest *may* be lodged."

Just then, the phone on the official's desk rang, interrupting the stalemate between East and West. Listening attentively to the party on the other end of the phone, the immigration supervisor only uttered a few words in Russian from time to time. Apparently, the other party was doing most of the talking. Completing the call, the officer put down the receiver, turned to the two Americans, and advised: "Okay, no problem. The ministry requires another paper [official document] to be issued to Mr. Jitter. Then, he will be cleared for entry."

Moving to an old manual typewriter that was set up in a corner of the office, the supervisor rolled a sheet of government stationery into the carriage. Striking the keys in two-finger fashion, the official took about five minutes to complete the paper. He then removed the document, signed it, and stamped it with an official seal. He folded the sheet and placed it inside Bob's passport. After handing the passport to Bob, the immigration supervisor cautioned both Americans: "Mr. *Jitter* must keep this paper with his passport until he departs the Soviet Union. The paper will be surrendered upon exit." With a sly grin, the immigration officer peered at Bob and proclaimed: "You may now proceed to customs. Welcome to the U.S.S.R."

On the way to the customs area, the assistant RSO looked over the document Bob was being required to carry. "What does it say?" Bob asked.

"Something about your passport being in error and that your true name is Robert Jitter."

"You're kidding!"

"No, the Russians aren't going to admit they made a mistake. And they might have done it on purpose to irritate us," remarked the assistant RSO.

Whether it was Soviet bureaucratic bungling or KGB (U.S.S.R. state security) gamesmanship, Bob had been officially renamed. For hotel and travel accommodations, on guest lists, at meetings, and the like, Bob was both listed and addressed by the Soviets as Robert *Jitter*—for the entire visit.

In those days, official visitors to the U.S.S.R. were tightly controlled. Accommodations were handled by the Ministry of Foreign Affairs, and the Seventh Directorate of the KGB closely monitored the movements of official guests. The Kissinger advance team was assigned rooms at the Sovietskaya, the official hotel of the Soviet Union. Located in the northern section of Moscow, the hotel was about a 10-minute drive to the Kremlin (seat of government). The Sovietskaya was erected in 1952 during the regime of Josef Stalin. Designed in a grand empire style, the hotel featured elegant-crystal chandeliers—suspended from high ceilings that were supported by ornate-marble columns.

After checking into the Sovietskaya, the SY agents went to their rooms to unpack. It was then they discovered that a number of personal belongings were missing. Wool socks, casual jeans, athletic shoes, and logo T-shirts had been removed from their luggage. Embassy personnel suspected that the items had been stolen at the Moscow airport—by either airline employees or the KGB. A thriving Soviet black market existed on such Western goods.

For the missing socks, an emergency call was made to D.C. where replacements were shipped to the U.S. Embassy in Moscow via diplomatic pouch and courier. Until the articles arrived, several SY agents were seen walking around in shoes without socks during the cold Russian winter.

For Mrs. Kissinger's visit to the Soviet Union, the SY agents coordinated their efforts with Ralph Basham, the USSS lead advance agent. Whenever Mrs. Kissinger was with her husband, she fell under the Secret Service "protective umbrella." During those times, SY agents would interface with the USSS detail. The senior SY agent would work close proximity to Mrs. Kissinger, while the remaining SY agents would add an additional layer of protection outside the USSS protective perimeter.

A native of Owensboro, Kentucky, Basham was a friendly and extremely capable agent. Bob told me on several occasions how lucky he was to be able to work with the Secret Service agents and to learn firsthand the intricacies of executive protection.

For Bob, it was a pleasurable and enjoyable experience—despite the long hours and out-of-town travel. For me, it became a growing burden, as I had to assume a larger portion of the family duties—necessitated by Bob's increasing absence.

The morning after the SY advance team arrived at the Sovietskaya, Bob ran into Agent Basham in the lobby of the hotel. Basham flashed a smile at Bob and greeted him with a loud, "Good morning, Agent *Jitter*."

"So, you heard," Bob replied.

"Yes, and I also heard you think your room is bugged."

"Most definitely," Bob confirmed. "Last night, another agent came to my door, and we were talking quietly. Next, we hear this crackle come from the TV set in my room—like someone was turning up a scratchy volume control. The odd thing about it: The set was turned off, and I had unplugged it when I moved in."

"That seals it for me," Basham declared. "I'm going to ask the foreign ministry to switch us to the Hotel Rossiya. It's a modern tourist hotel and not as gloomy as this place.

"My guys have been experiencing problems too. One received calls from a woman inviting him to the bar for a drink. After he hung up on her several times, a man called and told the same guy he looked 'cute' and asked if they could get together. They think they can play with us. This crap has got to stop."

For the upcoming trip, the Soviet government offered Mrs. Kissinger an itinerary that included visits to Soviet cultural attractions. These movements were scheduled to coincide with the strategic arms limitation talks (SALT) that would be held in Moscow between Secretary Kissinger and high-ranking Soviet officials. Since Mrs. Kissinger would be visiting these sites without her husband, SY would be solely responsible for coordination of the U.S. advance preparations with Soviet authorities. One of the visits planned by the Soviets for Mrs. Kissinger was a trip to the city of Leningrad.

The city was founded in 1703 by Czar Peter the Great, who originally named it Saint Petersburg—after his patron saint. At the start of World War I, St. Petersburg was renamed Petrograd. With the death of Vladimir Lenin in 1924, Petrograd was changed to Leningrad in honor of the leader of the 1917 Russian Revolution and the first head of state of the Soviet Union. With the dissolution of the Soviet Union in 1991, the city changed its name back to St. Petersburg.

SY Agent Greg Bujac, with Bob assisting, was selected to conduct the Leningrad advance. Like Bob, Greg performed his duties in a no-nonsense manner.

As domestic flights within the Soviet Union were not up to international standards—cabins were not pressurized, and maintenance concerns were an issue—Greg and Bob were booked on the historic *Red Arrow*, the overnight train to Leningrad. The train departed Moscow's Leningrad Station each night at 11:55 p.m., arriving in Leningrad at 7:55 a.m. the following morning.

Greg and Bob arrived at Lenigradsky Vokzal (Leningrad Station). The classically designed structure was built in the mid-1800s. The two agents moved to the platform area where a conductor checked tickets and directed the duo to one of the dark-red sleeper cars of the *Krasnya Strela* (*Red Arrow*).

Boarding the train, Bob and Greg immediately smelled the odor of burning charcoal emanating from the large copper samovar (urn to heat water) located at the end of the car. After making some cups of tea, the men located their compartment and sat down on the berths, which had already been made-up for sleeping. The two enjoyed the hot beverage, while they discussed some of the *unclassified* aspects of the Leningrad advance. Soon, the train pulled out of the station. The sleeper car rolled and pitched as the train was brought up to speed. The clack of the wheels resonated into the compartment, while the train whizzed by the snowy Russian countryside.

"What do you say, Bob? Let's hit the sack. We've got a long day ahead of us."

"I'm for that," Bob agreed.

Both travelers stripped down to their underwear. Greg turned off the lights. Our boys crawled into the berths and pulled up their covers. About five minutes later, there was a knock on the compartment door. "I'll get it," Greg bellowed. Sliding out of bed, Greg retrieved his glasses, which lay nearby. He cracked the door open and was surprised by a beautiful, young blonde, who tried to force her way into the compartment. "Hold it, sister," Greg commanded as he braced the door. "This compartment is occupied."

Pushing a ticket through the door opening, the blonde responded in English: "I have a ticket. Please let me in."

"No, we have the tickets for all the berths. You need to see the conductor. Good night," Greg told the blonde as he pushed the door closed and relocked it. Greg turned toward Bob and stated emphatically: "We're both married. She's not spending the night in here!"

About five minutes later, there was another knock at the door. This time, Greg didn't move from his berth but shouted out, with some annoyance, "Who's there?"

A voice answered: "Ingrid Andersen. The conductor said the train is full. Please let me in."

"No, we bought tickets for all four of the berths, so we'd have some privacy," Greg replied. "The conductor checked our tickets earlier. Look, we need to get some sleep."

Several minutes later, the door to the compartment flew open. The conductor had used his passkey to unlock the door. The attractive blonde rushed into the compartment, carrying an overnight bag in one hand and a ticket in the other. Greg and Bob jumped out of the berths and put their trousers on.

"Wait a minute," Greg asserted. "This isn't right." Greg grabbed his and Bob's tickets and snatched the ticket from the blonde's hand. Greg moved to the corridor of the train to resolve the matter with the conductor.

In the meantime, the statuesque blonde advanced toward Bob. In a soft, sensuous voice she pleaded: "Please let me stay with you. I'm alone and frightened." She then retrieved a passport from her coat pocket and showed it to Bob. "It's okay," the blonde added. "I'm not Russian; I'm Swedish. I'm traveling back to Stockholm." Bob understood the assertion since U.S. personnel were not permitted to fraternize with Soviet nationals.

"I'm sorry," Bob replied. "You can't stay here."

"Let me stay with you—*please*." Shaking his head, Bob escorted the blonde outside to the corridor where Greg was making his case.

The conductor understood some English but seemed reluctant to become involved. Pointing to the ticket in question, Greg reiterated to the conductor: "This lady's ticket is for another compartment. Will you please help her?" The conductor finally took the blonde's ticket, examined it, and grumbled something in Russian. He then motioned to the blonde. With a look of dejection, the attractive blond stranger followed the conductor down the corridor of the train. Bob and Greg returned to their berths where they slept uninterrupted for the remainder of the night.

The next morning, they were met at the train station by the security officer from the U.S. Consulate General, which opened in Leningrad in 1973. Consulates foster trade and handle the interests of visiting Americans. They are located in popular tourist cities and cities of commerce. While there might be several U.S. consulates in a foreign country, there will be only one U.S. Embassy. The embassy will be located in the foreign nation's capital. The embassy provides a full-range of administrative services and is led by an ambassador, who serves as the official U.S. representative to the foreign government.

At the Leningrad Consulate, Bob and Greg were ushered into a "safe room" where they would brief the consul general on Mrs. Kissinger's upcoming visit. Safe rooms in U.S. embassies and consulates are really rooms within a room. They are designed to protect conversations from eavesdropping. The interior walls, floor, and ceiling of the outer room are removed to eliminate hiding places for listening devices. The inner room is constructed entirely of plexiglass. This allows one to easily see that no "bugs" have been inserted into either of the rooms. The plastic enclosure also acts as a sound attenuator.

Security advances were completed and the Kissingers arrived in Moscow. While Secretary Kissinger hammered away at SALT and the proposed Vladivostok Summit between President Ford and Secretary General Brezhnev, Mrs. Kissinger took VIP tours hosted by the Soviet government. She visited the cathedrals and palaces of the Kremlin (old citadel of the city), the Bolshoi Ballet, Red Square and Lenin's Tomb, the czar's bell and cannon, and other famous sites.

In Leningrad, Mrs. Kissinger visited the State Hermitage Museum and the palaces of the czars. Mrs. Kissinger was told at the Hermitage; if she spent one minute at each exhibit it would take about 11 years to complete the tour. Fortunately for Bob and the other SY agents, Mrs. Kissinger opted for an abbreviated visit.

She only asked to see some of the magnificent paintings along with Fabergé eggs and the imperial crown jewels.

When I heard all that Bob was able to see, I was a bit envious and really wished that I could have been there with him. I knew Bob was enjoying the sightseeing aspect of his work. In college, he had selected courses in the humanities and art for electives. It was certainly a golden opportunity to see things that the rest of us can only dream about.

With the Kissingers departure from the Soviet Union, the U.S. Embassy held a "wheels up" party at the restaurant/bar atop the Rossiya Hotel in Moscow. Greg Bujac and Bob stopped by to give thanks to all who had assisted with the visit. The embassy also invited the Soviet officials who had hosted the trip. One of the Soviets attending was a Russian KGB colonel, whom Bob and Greg had met during the visit.

The SY agents had been told by their Soviet counterparts that the colonel neither understood nor spoke any English. Throughout the trip, Bob and Greg had to use an interpreter to converse with the colonel. Now, he was bellied up to the bar and enjoying straight double shots of Stolichnaya vodka. When he saw Bob and Greg, the colonel cheerily called out: "Hello, my American friends. Please come and enjoy some good Russian vodka with me."

Bob responded with a grin, "Colonel, I don't know who your English teacher is, but they sure have done a good job with you in only a couple of days."

Greg added: "Yeah, colonel, I guess we don't need to find an interpreter. Thanks for the help you gave us."

The colonel's face filled with mirth as he let out a hearty laugh. "You two are funny guys. And Mr. *Jitter* is a good sport. I like Americans. It was my pleasure to help you."

Then, the KGB colonel pointed to the upper-level mezzanine of the room. "Why didn't you like my sweetie?" he asked. Leaning over the railing was the beautiful blond stranger, who had tried to spend the night with Bob and Greg onboard the *Red Arrow*. She smiled and waved to our boys.

"Don't blame her, colonel," Bob replied. "She's got the curves, but we're both happily married and love our wives."

"And we're not that lucky—for it not to have been a setup," added Greg.

From Moscow, the Kissingers traveled to India. Bob leap-frogged to Tehran, Iran with SY Agent Tim Robinson and USSS Lead Advance Agent Ralph Basham. In 1974, Iran was ruled by Shah Mohammed Reza Pahlavi (Shah of Iran). SAVAK, the Iranian secret police, controlled internal security. Former CIA Director Richard Helms was the U.S. ambassador to Iran. U.S. arms sales to Iran totaled in the billions of dollars. A large American advisory group trained the Iranian military in the use and maintenance of the weapons.

In spite of the iron hand of SAVAK, there was a guerilla movement operating in Iran that wanted to overthrow the shah and drive out the U.S. presence. Traveling in Iran was not without risk—if you were an American official. Former U.S. Ambassador Douglas MacArthur II and his wife escaped a kidnapping attempt in 1971. Four armed men stopped the ambassador's car and attempted to break out the windows with an ax. The ambassador's driver managed to pull away from the attackers. In 1972, a U.S. Air Force brigadier general was seriously wounded when he drove over a bomb, and in 1973 a U.S. Army lieutenant colonel was assassinated while traveling to work.

Trying not to become a target of opportunity, Bob sought authorization to rent a foreign car for his and Tim's travel to Isfahan, Shiraz, and Persepolis for the SY advance. When that request was turned down as being too costly, Bob asked for a nondescript car from the embassy motor pool.

The following morning, an embassy car with driver arrived at Bob and Tim's hotel. The vehicle was a late model four-door Chevrolet sedan, black in color. The driver wore black pants, a white shirt with black tie, and a black cap. Not only was the vehicle displaying diplomatic license plates, an American flag was flying from the right front fender! Tim Robinson asked the embassy driver, an English-speaking Iranian national, "Don't you have something a little less official looking?"

"No, all embassy cars the same," answered the driver.

"Well, please take the flag down," Tim directed. "We're trying not to draw attention to ourselves."

The driver moved close to Tim and stated in a low voice, "I understand—you CIA."

"No, no, no!" Tim burst out. "We're just helping with the Kissingers' visit."

While the embassy driver removed the American flag, Bob jumped behind the wheel. Tim slid in the right front seat and rode "shotgun." Bob called out to the driver: "Get in the back; I'm driving. You're going to see what it's like to be chauffeured around." As a driver for Mrs. Kissinger, Bob had received specialized training in breaking blockades and other scenarios regarding attacks on motor vehicles by terrorists. If something was going to happen, Bob didn't want to trust his and Tim's life to a motor pool driver.

Bob and Tim drove south from Tehran through the arid Iranian desert—with the embassy driver serving as guide and translator. Over 200 miles later, they pulled into the Iranian city of Isfahan. The city had its origins thousands of years ago and had been the capital of Persia during the 16th century. Isfahan featured many marvelous sites of Islamic architecture, culture, and history. Its palaces, mosques, gardens, fountains, and bridges reflected the ancient Persian expression: "Esfahan nesf-e Jahan" (Isfahan is half the world).

The U.S. Embassy had reserved a room for Bob and Tim at an Isfahan hotel. The hotel had quite an unusual feature. Like something out of *Arabian Nights*, the entry doors to the guest rooms were arch shaped with an open area both above and below the door. The distance between the floor and the bottom of the door was several feet. This allowed anyone so inclined to gain entry into the room by simply crawling under the door. Our boys were a bit uncomfortable upon retiring for the evening.

The night passed without incident, and the next morning Bob was on his way to Shiraz and Persepolis to conduct the advance along with USSS Agent Ralph Basham. Persepolis was the center of the Persian Empire from about 518 B.C. to 330 B.C. when the city was plundered and burned by Alexander the Great. Eventually, Persepolis was abandoned. Its ruins were first studied in the 1930s when archaeologists from the University of Chicago began excavations. Among the remains were massive stone columns and buildings. The buildings, terraces, gates, and walls featured bas-reliefs and colossuses.

At the conclusion of the Persepolis visit, Bob was able to catch a ride back to Tehran with Ralph Basham via an Imperial Iranian Air Force helicopter. This would save many hours of driving through desolate and possibly dangerous territory.

A Secret Service agent, who had been assisting in the southern Iranian advance, also wanted to take the chopper rather than ride in an embassy car the almost 450 miles to Tehran. On his way to Persepolis from Shiraz, the agent radioed Basham to hold the aircraft. Ralph smiled at Bob and playfully said, "Watch this." Basham transmitted back: "The chopper captain wants to leave immediately. What's your ETA?"

"Ralph, I should be there in about 15. Please tell him to wait!"

"Standby, I'll talk with the captain." A minute later Ralph transmitted again: "You better tell your driver to pick it up, son. I could only get the captain to wait another five minutes. He says there's a dust storm brewing over the desert, and we'll have to leave in five—with or without you."

"Ralph, we're hitting top end now! Stall 'em!"

Holding back his laughter, Basham answered: "I'll try, partner. But I don't control the Iranian air force."

Just then, Bob and Ralph saw a cloud of dust appear on the road—far off in the distance. "That must be him," Bob said to Ralph.

The five minutes expired and like clockwork, Basham raised the radio to mouth level. To simulate a message from an airborne helicopter, he continuously squeezed the transmitter key on and off while talking. Basham radioed that he couldn't hold the chopper any longer and that he and Bob were en route to Tehran.

"Ralph, you're breaking up. Don't leave me! Don't leave me!" boomed from out of Basham's radio.

The agent finally arrived and found the helicopter still on the ground with Ralph, Bob, and the Iranian flight crew beaming with laughter. "Damn it, Ralph! You almost gave me a heart attack!" yelled the agent—still frantic with worry.

After the Iranian trip, Bob was able to come home for a while. In addition to backgrounds and being a regular temp with the Mrs. K. detail, Bob was now being assigned passport and visa fraud investigations. Being selected to conduct criminal investigations was advancement for Bob. He dove back into his investigations, but soon Bob was needed for yet another out-of-town, protective assignment. He headed to New York with Tim Robinson to provide protection for Imelda Marcos.

For the 1974 United Nations General Assembly (UNGA), the secretary of state designated a number of attendees as "official guests" to the U.S. These high-profile dignitaries did not qualify for statutory USSS protection. One was Imelda Marcos, the wife of Philippine President Ferdinand Marcos. As first lady of the Philippines, Mrs. Marcos had survived an assassination attempt carried out by Carlito Dimailig, a 27-year-old geodetic engineer. The incident took place on December 7, 1972, and was caught "live" on Filipino television.

Mrs. Marcos was presenting beautification awards during a ceremony in Manila. As one group of recipients was leaving the presentation area, Dimailig came up on stage and approached Mrs. Marcos. Filipinos watched in horror as the would-be assassin pulled a 12-inch bolo knife from his sleeve and began to slash at Mrs. Marcos. She turned and put her arms up to block the blows—then collapsed to the stage. Agents of the Presidential Security Force rushed to her aid, fatally shooting Dimailig.

Mrs. Marcos was evacuated by helicopter. At the hospital, she received 75 stitches to her right arm.

In November of 1974, Mrs. Marcos was officially traveling to New York for the UNGA and to open the new Philippine Center, which was located at 556 Fifth Avenue in Manhattan. This visit presented some memorable moments for the agents of SY.

For the Marcos arrival at JFK airport, Tim Robinson was the "baggage agent." His duties included securing Mrs. Marcos' luggage and transporting it to the Carlyle Hotel where the Marcos party would be staying. Located on the Upper East Side of Manhattan, the art deco designed Carlyle dates back to 1930. It's New York's posh hotel for the world's elite.

Assigned to the follow-up car, Bob stood on the tarmac with Tim as the Philippine Air Force (PAF) plane pulled to its parking point and the engines were shut down. Stairs were pulled to the aircraft, and its door opened. A pair of PAF airmen scrambled off and proceeded to open compartments in the underbelly of the plane in order to offload Mrs. Marcos' luggage. Tim walked over to inform them that a station wagon was standing by for the luggage transport. One of the airmen looked over at the station wagon and asked, "Is that the only vehicle you have for baggage?"

"Yes," Tim replied in a worried tone.

The airman chuckled as he told Tim, "The first lady has 75 pieces of luggage that need to go to the Carlyle."

"What!" Tim cried out in disbelief.

"You're lucky," stated the airman. "She's traveling with 150 pieces. Half of them are empty for any purchases she might make. We'll keep them on board until she needs them." Tim had to go back to the terminal and rent a box truck for the transport.

The second surprise to the SY detail came with Mrs. Marcos' schedule. Bob, Tim, and several other SY agents were assigned to the night shift; most protective personnel were scheduled for the day shift, which included two NYPD detectives. The "skeleton" night shift arrived at 8:00 p.m. to find the day crew sitting around bored and restless. "What did you guys do today?" Bob asked.

"Nothing," answered the detail leader. "We sat here all day. She must be recovering from her travel. There's nothing on her schedule. Looks like you men will have a quiet night."

About 30 minutes after the day shift left, an aide to Mrs. Marcos appeared from within the suite with a list of expected guests. Included were such notable names as pianist Van Cliburn and artist Andy Warhol. The guests arrived, and at about 10:45 p.m. the aide returned to announce, "Mrs. Marcos and her guests will be going out for the evening."

Bob was on the front door post and thought the aide was joking. Realizing the aide was serious, Bob advised: "We'll want to have an agent advance the locations. Can you please tell us where we'll be going?"

"Copacabana, Delmonico's, '21' Club, and possibly other nightspots."

The SY detail quickly made arrangements for the unscheduled movements. Later that night and into the next day, Mrs. Marcos and her guests visited several New York clubs—ending up at the '21' Club. There, Mrs. Marcos, who had a lovely voice, sang until the wee hours of the morning—accompanied by Van Cliburn on piano. Mrs. Marcos arrived back at the Carlyle at 6:30 a.m.

The day shift checked in at 7:45 a.m., and the detail leader joked, "How much sleep did you guys get last night?"

The night shift supervisor answered: "None! We just got back. We were out all night."

The detail leader laughed and said, "Yeah, right."

The next day was almost an exact repeat. Mrs. Marcos slept and stayed in her suite during the day. Guests arrived between 9:00 p.m. and 10:00 p.m. Then Mrs. Marcos and her guests would spend all night on the town. The night supervisor finally convinced the detail leader that it wasn't a joke, and shift personnel were adjusted to Mrs. Marcos' New York lifestyle.

There was some excitement during the visit. On Monday afternoon, November 18, 1974, the phone in Bob and Tim's hotel room rang. It was the detail leader instructing them to report to the CP immediately. There, Bob, Tim, and the rest of the detail were briefed on an incident that had just occurred in Washington, D.C.

Napoleon Lechoco, a Philippine émigré to the U.S., had taken over the Philippine chancery (office building) at 1617 Massachusetts Avenue, NW. Lechoco was a leader of the Filipino community in the D.C. Metropolitan Area. As a ploy, he had made an appointment with the Philippine ambassador, Eduardo Romualdez. Once Lechoco gained access to the ambassador's office, he pulled a handgun from a briefcase. In the commotion, an economic attaché was shot and presumed dead. Lechoco then handcuffed Ambassador Romualdez—holding him hostage at gunpoint.

In New York, the night shift agents were being called in early to provide additional security for Mrs. Marcos in case there was a wider plot. And since the Philippine ambassador had been seized and the chancery evacuated, the U.S. Department of State had been asked by the FBI to establish contact with the Philippine government. Because Bob had been a police officer in D.C. and was familiar with the area, he was asked to serve as liaison between SY and Mrs. Marcos' security aide.

Authorities in D.C. talked with Lechoco via telephone for the purpose of negotiating the subject's surrender and the safe release of the ambassador. In New York, Bob briefed the security aide and Mrs. Marcos on the situation. Mrs. Marcos immediately expressed her deep concern for Ambassador Romualdez, who was also Mrs. Marcos' uncle.

As the evening progressed, it was learned that Lechoco and his wife had immigrated to the U.S. in 1972—without their children. In October 1974, six of the seven Lechoco children were permitted to leave the Philippines to rejoin their parents, who resided in Oxon Hill, Maryland. Mr. Lechoco was under the impression that his oldest child, a 17-year-old son, was being detained in the Philippines. Thus, Lechoco demanded that his son be allowed to leave the Philippines, so he could travel to the U.S.

Although the press reported that President Marcos had played the major role for the Philippine government during the crisis, Bob knew firsthand that Mrs. Marcos had actually made the decisions from New York. Mrs. Marcos had dispatched Philippine diplomats from New York to Washington to standby on the scene. She also directed her youngest brother, Benjamin Romualdez, to travel from Manila to Washington to assist in the negotiations—in case the incident became drawn out.

Later that night, however, Mrs. Marcos promised the following: If Lechoco would give himself up and release the ambassador unharmed, Lechoco's son would be granted an immediate exit visa and put on the next flight to the United States.

In the early morning hours of Tuesday, November 19, Lechoco threw his gun out a second-floor window of the four-story brick building nestled along Washington's Embassy Row. Lechoco and Ambassador Romualdez appeared moments later. In a fortunate surprise, they were followed by Mario Lagdemeo—the economic attaché who was thought to have been killed. He had only received a flesh wound and had feigned death during the ordeal. Mrs. Marcos was overjoyed with the good news.

Lechoco was taken into custody by the FBI and sent to St. Elizabeths Hospital for a psychiatric evaluation. Found competent to stand trial, Lechoco was convicted in 1975 of kidnapping and sentenced to 10 years in prison. Subsequently, Lechoco won an appeal for a new trial. In 1977, he was acquitted by a jury that found him "not guilty by reason of insanity." Released unconditionally, Lechoco became a free man.

Mrs. Marcos and her security aide were grateful for the help given by Bob during the incident. To show thanks, the security aide invited Bob into one of the outer rooms of the Marcos suite. Mrs. Marcos adored fresh-cut flowers. The room was literally filled with floral arrangements sent by Mrs. Marcos' many personal and official friends. The aide invited Bob to select an arrangement to give to me. Bob declined the gracious offer by saying: "Thanks very much. But I'm from out of town. So, I really couldn't get them home to her."

"Then pick out one of the vases for your wife," the aide suggested.

Bob looked around the room and saw a metal vase in the corner. "Okay, thanks. I'll take that metal one. I'd be afraid the ceramic and crystal ones might break in my suitcase."

The aide went to the vase, removed the flowers, and emptied the water into another container. "Here you go, Mr. Bob—with our thanks."

Bob took the vase to his hotel room and placed it in one of his suitcases—not thinking much more about it. The next morning after being relieved from duty, Bob got some breakfast and then went to bed. Several hours later, he's awakened from a sound sleep by some furious pounding on his room door. Bob opened the door and found the Philippine security aide with a very worried look on his face.

"Mr. Bob, I'm sorry, but I need the vase back! I found out it was an official state gift to the first lady from the Saudi Arabian ambassador to the U.N. It's handcrafted from *solid silver* by artisans to the royal family! The ambassador mentioned it in a phone call to the first lady. The ambassador is coming for lunch. We need the vase for the table setting."

"Sure, I understand. Let me get it."

"Mr. Bob, I'm sorry about this. With all the flower arrangements arriving daily for the first lady, the significance of this one was not caught by our staff. Of course, you're welcome to pick another vase for your wife." When Bob returned home after his detail assignment, he told the story, as he presented me a heavy, cut-crystal vase. I had a good laugh.

Bob gained much valuable experience at Park Police and the Department of State. He didn't just want to be a good Secret Service agent; he wanted to be one of the best! Bob was on a noble mission, and failure was *not* an option.

Chapter 6

Secret Service

UNITED STATES SECRET SERVICE
TREASURY DEPARTMENT
ROBERT RITTER
Special Agent

is commissioned by the United States Secret Service, Treasury Department, to protect the President of the United States and others as authorized by statute; to detect and arrest any person violating federal laws relating to coins, obligations, and securities of the United States and foreign governments, and in performance of these duties, to arrest any person committing any offense against the United States. This person has Top Secret Clearance and is commended to those with whom official business is conducted as worthy of trust and confidence.

When Bob entered the U.S. Secret Service on January 6, 1975, he was already an experienced investigator and protection agent. At the Washington Field Office (WFO), he was assigned background investigations and immediately stood post for protective movements. Bob's *first* USSS protective assignment was a visit by President Gerald Ford to the Washington Hilton Hotel.

Bob was posted outdoors at the T Street side of the hotel. The site advance agent briefed Bob as to the duties of the post. This area contained VIP and public entrances. President Ford would be arriving by motorcade at the VIP entrance. This entrance opened into a private area, which housed an elevator and a spiral stairway. One floor down, a corridor led to the stage entrance of the ballroom.

The T Street public entrance led into the terrace level of the hotel. From this level, guests could access the other floors of the hotel via stairways and elevators. Both public and VIP entrances were accessed by a single driveway and sidewalk that were just off T Street.

T Street had been posted earlier with "Emergency No Parking" signs. Now, T Street was being closed between Connecticut and Florida Avenues. A rope line had been set along the sidewalk to block entry into the presidential arrival area and to funnel guests into the T Street public entrance.

Later that evening, an older agent stopped by Bob's post. The agent extended his hand and introduced himself. "I'm Bill Foster from Protective Forces."

"Glad to meet you, sir. I'm Bob Ritter."

"Bob, I've been told you just transferred from SY."

"Yes, sir, I was sworn in on Monday."

Foster broke a nervous laugh as he said: "This might be some kind of modern-day record—working presidential protection after only a couple of days on the job. What protective experience do you have?"

"I worked foreign dignitaries and Mrs. Kissinger's detail at State. Before that, I was a Park Police officer. I worked protective movements and at Camp David. I also walked the White House sidewalk, Ellipse, and Lafayette Park beats."

"Good," Foster said—looking a bit relieved. "Then you're familiar with the *basic* principle of Secret Service protection."

"It's a system of concentric security perimeters that provide 360-degree protection," Bob answered.

"That's right," Foster affirmed, looking even more relieved. "Keeping that in mind, what are the duties of your post?"

"I'm controlling access to the arrival area and observing everyone coming in and out of the hotel—looking for anyone suspicious. I'm also watching the windows in the building across the street. When we get near the time the presidential motorcade will depart the White House, the site advance agent will close this side of the sidewalk at Florida Avenue. An agent will secure the T Street public doors from the inside, so no one can come out who's not cleared. I'll be out here with MPD [Metropolitan Police Department] making sure this side of the street is clear of anyone who isn't authorized. The public area will then become a credentialed press area for the president's arrival. After the president is inside, we'll reopen this side of the sidewalk and the T Street public entrance. We'll close them back down again for the president's departure."

"Very good, nice meeting you, Bob, and good luck in your career," Foster said.

At Treasury agent school, Bob finished first in his class of 50 agents. Later that year after completion of Secret Service school, he was reassigned to the WFO Protective Intelligence Squad (PI).

Out of necessity, Bob was soon placed into the PI Squad duty agent mix. After hours, the WFO phone line was transferred to the Treasury Department switchboard. When an emergency call came in, the Treasury operator forwarded it to the WFO duty agent. That agent in turn notified the appropriate squad duty agent. The WFO duty agent and the squad duty agents were rotated on a weekly basis. There were only five agents in the PI Squad at the time. With agents out on TDY assignments and the like, Bob was frequently scheduled to be the agent on call for the PI Squad.

There were no pagers or cell phones. The WFO duty agent and squad duty agents were required to stay home at nights and on weekends. For most squads, it wasn't more than an occasional imposition. For the agents in PI, it was a relentless burden. Routinely, someone in the Washington area was coming to the protective attention of the Secret Service. It seemed that the nighttime brought out the PI subjects like stars in the sky. Our phone rang on many a late night and early morning. No matter how many times it happened, I never got used to it. Startled, I would awake nervous and uneasy. The ringing warned that Bob would soon be taken from my side and the safety of our home.

Jotting down the information, Bob planned his action accordingly. Then, Bob hurriedly got dressed, attaching his gun, handcuffs, radio, ammo case, and badge to his pants belt. For his badge, Bob had a special holder, which clipped to the belt. Wearing the badge to the left of the holster, Bob could flip back his suit coat to expose the badge when he identified himself to suspects. This kept the right hand near the holster in case Bob had to draw his weapon. Watching Bob put on the Secret Service star in the middle of the night always reminded me of the danger inherent in law enforcement. Sometimes I got back to sleep, and sometimes I lay restless—worrying about Bob as he disappeared into the darkness.

Many times, I didn't see Bob until the next evening. In spite of having to work all night on the new case, he was still expected to work his regular-day hours and assignments. All protective intelligence cases were important. Threat cases received the highest priority. Like homicide investigations, threats against Secret Service protectees were investigated immediately, and the cases were worked until a preliminary resolution could be attained.

Bob worked 36 hours straight on one *direct threat* case. These were cases where the subject clearly threatened (spoken or written) the president or other protectee. *Indirect* or *conditional threats* were dependent on stipulations and marked with uncertainty. Examples of indirect threats are as follows: (1) If the president doesn't change his ways, he will be struck down, (2) I might shoot the president if he gets us in another war, and (3) If the president were here, I'd punch him in the nose.

Conditional threat cases were not prosecuted by the U.S. Attorney's Office unless agents could show that the subject *intended* to inflict bodily harm. An element of the crime (18 U.S.C. Section 871) was that threats had to be made "knowingly and willfully." In 1969, the U.S. Supreme Court decided in Watts v. United States (394 U.S. 705) that appellant's statement, "If they ever make me carry a rifle, the first man I want to get in my sights is L.B.J.," was not a true threat. The Supreme Court remanded the case back to the U.S. Court of Appeals with a judgment for acquittal.

The Supreme Court reasoned that the subject made the statement in the context of an anti-war rally and that it was "political hyperbole." The court also noted the conditionality of the statement: The subject would first have to be drafted into the Army. It was ruled that political hyperbole, words spoken in jest, and idle talk were constitutionally protected speech.

Mental illness, lack of intent, the inability to carry out the threat, and intoxication were other prime factors used by assistant U.S. attorneys in deciding the prosecutorial merit of threat cases. Bob spent many a night tracking down subjects who had engaged in "bar talk" of a threatening nature toward the president or other protectee. Most of the time, the subjects claimed they had been intoxicated and didn't mean what they had said. One was a soldier of fortune wannabe, who had tried to impress the ladies.

Bob took all of these cases seriously. He remembered that Samuel Byck had been reported to the Secret Service for sounding off in a bar. It was alleged that Byck had said words to the effect that someone should kill President Nixon. Byck ended up trying to assassinate Nixon in a bizarre aircraft-hijacking attempt where he planned to crash the plane into the White House. Even though Byck's "Operation Pandora's Box" never got off the ground, Byck killed two innocent people before committing suicide during the failed attempt.

Since the president resided at the White House, all roads led to Washington for protective intelligence subjects who were having mental episodes. Those who didn't have cars most often traveled to D.C. via bus or train. These modes of transportation were cheaper than air travel. PI subjects were commonly out of work and low on funds. In some of these cases, the Secret Service was tipped off to the subject's travel to Washington. Bob was regularly called to intercept these subjects upon their arrival in D.C.

A major portal to the city was the Greyhound Bus Terminal at 1110 New York Avenue, NW. Built in 1940 of limestone over reinforced concrete, the structure was a striking example of art deco architecture. The nearby Trailways Terminal (1200 I Street, NW) was the other major bus gateway to Washington. Between the two facilities, hundreds of buses arrived daily.

Traveling by rail, PI subjects disembarked at Washington's magnificent Union Station. Designed in a Beau Arts classical style, the station opened in 1907. Constructed of marble and granite, the building featured a grand facade with columns and arches, 96-foot-high vaulted ceilings, colossal statues, and other allegorical adornment.

During the golden age of railroading, Union Station was one of the busiest terminals in the nation and saw its share of presidential arrivals and departures. In fact, the station was designed with a presidential suite, which offered safe access and security. This innovation was the result of President James A. Garfield's 1881 assassination. Garfield was shot while walking through the waiting room of Washington's old Baltimore and Potomac Railroad Station. Although the suite at Union Station hadn't been used by a president since Eisenhower's time, it stood as a reminder to Bob of the potential danger a president faced when traversing a public area.

The 18 tracks and platforms of Union Station handled hundreds of trains and many thousands of passengers a day. The station's grand concourse was big enough to hold the Washington Monument if laid on its side. In those days, passengers were not required to give names or show identification when purchasing tickets. It was a difficult and time-consuming task to intercept persons of interest unless detailed travel information was available.

Often, PI subjects made their way to the White House or to a site that the president might be visiting. PI subjects also telephoned the White House and mailed letters to the president. Even though these appearances and communications might not be overtly threatening, they could still earn a Secret Service interview if bizarre behavior, irrational ideas, or an insistence to gain personal access to the president was exhibited.

Bob spent several years in the PI Squad and had many important cases and assignments including Washington area PI coordinator for the American Revolution Bicentennial Celebration. As the WFO bicentennial coordinator, Bob was tasked with establishing intelligence contacts and developing meaningful information to ensure USSS protectees would be safe during the celebration. For the months leading up to the bicentennial, Bob worked many hours "staying ahead of the intelligence curve" as he called it. He even established intelligence contacts with police in New York, Chicago, Miami, South Dakota, and Puerto Rico.

Bob believed the WFO-PI squad to be the busiest and most important in the country. During his tenure, he also researched presidential assassinations and assassins, while coining a new saying: "Desperate people are dangerous people."

Bob's study yielded some interesting statistics. During the period 1835–1976, there were 13 assassination attempts with a direction of interest toward the office of the presidency. Of those 13 attempts, nine were made on sitting presidents, and three took place against presidential candidates. The other incident targeted a president-elect.

Easily concealable handguns were used in 11 of the 13 attempts. Eight of the handgun attempts were made at close range. Two other pistol attacks occurred at ranges of approximately 30 and 40 feet. The other handgun assault took place on the sidewalk in front of Blair House. A rifle was utilized in one of the assassination attempts. In another, a commercial airliner was the intended weapon.

Five of the 13 attempts were successful. Four presidents (Lincoln, Garfield, McKinley, and JFK) and one presidential candidate (RFK) were assassinated. Two of the 13 attempts were partially successful in that targeted principals were wounded

(Theodore Roosevelt and George Wallace). Handguns were used in six of the seven attempts that were either successful or partially successful.

In the 13 attempts that Bob examined, six others also lost their lives—including two law enforcement officers, two bystanders, and two perpetrators. A Puerto Rican terrorist was fatally shot by a mortally wounded White House policeman during the 1950 Truman assassination attempt. And in 1974, Samuel Byck committed suicide during his failed attempt.

Although Secret Service protection was in effect during eight of the 13 attempts, in only two instances did Secret Service agents and/or police fire weapons. That was during the 1950 assault on Blair House and the initial stage of the 1974 attempt by Samuel Byck.

After an analysis of these past events, Bob disclosed an alarming prediction for the future. "It's *more likely* the next presidential assassination attempt will be by a lone gunman using a handgun at close range," he told me. "It will probably happen in or near a public area, and the subject will be waiting to strike. And the scary part: The Service doesn't have a reliable method to prevent it from happening."

Believing a *behavioral* assessment of subjects was more accurate than agents' gut feelings, Bob developed a point-weighted checklist he titled the Protective Interest Evaluation Review (PIER). It compared the actions of his case subjects with those of known assassins. He submitted it as an employee suggestion, but his supervisor would not forward it to headquarters.

Bob used techniques and strategies that he devised when he could, but the Assistant to the Special Agent in Charge (ATSAIC or AT) of the PI Squad would not implement them. Bob was simply told that he needed to eventually get reassigned to the Service's Intelligence Division (ID) where he could present his ideas directly to proper authorities.

Suggestions included the use of a PI Command Post folder for protectee visits, procedures for surveilling and working a crowd at checkpoints and public areas, and assigning two PI teams to presidential protective movements instead of the USSS practice of only one. Bob developed and honed these techniques, while he was assigned to conduct PI advances throughout the 1976 presidential primaries and fall campaign.

Bob called from the road and related how his ideas were being well received by state and local law-enforcement personnel. I was proud of him. In 1972, he theorized ways of improving executive protection. Four years later, Bob was actually putting his ideas into action.

During one Southern advance, Bob arrived in town and was told by police that an explosive device had been found in the city's auditorium—several days before. The device had been deactivated without injury. The police believed the bomb had been placed due to a labor dispute. They were convinced it had no direction of interest to the impending presidential candidate's visit.

Still, Bob didn't want to take any chances. He immediately notified the lead advance agent and the Intelligence Division. Next, Bob anxiously awaited the arrival of the EOD (Explosive Ordinance Demolition) team assigned to the visit, to inform them of the news. Bob had worked with this particular team on prior advances. The team leader was an Army sergeant first class, who was a couple of months from retirement. He was a short timer, who was looking forward to life after the military. The other team member was a young corporal, who carried the bags and did all the heavy lifting.

Bob was waiting for the team as they pulled up to the entrance of the hotel where the advance party was staying. It was a warm, sunny day and the front windows of the team's rental car were down. The corporal was driving, while the sergeant sat relaxed in the passenger's seat, blowing smoke from a dollar cigar and looking more like a chauffeured millionaire. These were good assignments for enlisted personnel. EOD teams in support of the Secret Service wore civilian clothes, flew commercially, drove rental cars, and stayed in major hotels.

Leaning out the window, the sergeant greeted Bob with a broad smile and a handshake. Bob got right to business. "Men, we need to check out an explosive device that was found at the civic center. It's ..."

Before Bob could finish, the sergeant began to wail like a wounded boar: "Oh—sh-t! Only 57 days to retirement. I should have stayed in the office. No, I had to hit the friggin' road! Serves me right. Oh, sh-t!" The sergeant then turned to the corporal and barked, "Son, when we get there, you grab the equipment and do exactly like I tell you."

"Sarge, settle down!" Bob stated with authority. "The device was found a couple of days ago. It was made safe by the sheriff's department. It's at the bomb squad's office. I want us to look at it for technical details. Then we can go to the civic center to see exactly where it was found. Afterwards, I need to get a teletype out to headquarters."

"Oh, okay—understood," the sergeant said, gaining some composure. The junior member of the team just shook his head.

During the Illinois primary, Bob worked Ronald Reagan's visit to the northern part of the state. The advance team did an early morning check in at a hotel in Waukegan, Illinois (on the shore of Lake Michigan) and then headed out to conduct the advance. It was off-season and the hotel was just about deserted. When they returned that evening, a television crew was set up out front. The lobby was bristling with activity, and people were waiting to be seated in the restaurant of the hotel. "What's going on?" Bob asked a pair of ladies, who were sitting in the lobby.

"The Secret Service is staying here for Ronnie Reagan's visit," one of the gals answered excitedly. "It's been all over the radio and TV. We thought we'd come on over and check it out. Who are you with?"

"Just a traveling salesman," Bob answered. Apparently, not much happened in Waukegan during those days.

An especially moving moment occurred between Bob and me during the North Carolina primary. Bob called late one night from Asheville, North Carolina. He had just finished working

Ronald and Nancy Reagan's visit to the Biltmore House. George W. Vanderbilt, an heir to railroad magnate Cornelius Vanderbilt, built the home in the 1890s. Designed after French Renaissance chateaus, the four-story brick mansion features a 780-foot facade and 250 rooms. It stands on a 125,000-acre estate in the western mountains of North Carolina.

Recounting the candlelight tour, Bob said the Reagans looked like "a couple on their honeymoon." Their eyes "sparkled with romance." Bob could see the deep love the Reagans had for each other. Bob said it reminded him of our love. I told Bob I loved him and asked him to be safe. "The toughest thing I face every day is being away from you and the kids," Bob declared. Bob touched my heart. I missed him very much.

Bob kept busy in the primaries and was occasionally called out at night. In one instance, he drove over a hundred miles to a highway patrol station for an important investigation. A person had given a statement to police regarding a plot by two unknown subjects to assassinate President Gerald Ford. The individual had been found along the side of the interstate by a highway patrolman. Claiming to have escaped with his life, the subject exhibited evidence of having been beaten. A national lookout was issued.

Bob arrived and began an intensive interview with the complainant. Concerned with certain parts of the story, Bob continued the questioning for several hours. Finally, the interviewee admitted he had made-up the part about the assassination plot. In reality, the complainant was hitchhiking when he was picked up by two males. The two unknown subjects were sharply critical of President Ford but made no threats. A fight broke out between the hitchhiker and one of the subjects. The car was stopped, and the hitchhiker was thrown from the vehicle. Angry with the subjects, the complainant decided to "really get back at them."

One call from Bob in early 1976 did foreshadow a momentous event yet to come. Bob had just watched the movie *Taxi Driver* on the pay-for-view in his hotel room. The Martin Scorsese directed film starred Robert De Niro as Travis Bickle, a mentally disturbed Vietnam War veteran. Actress Cybill Shepherd's screen role was that of Betsy, a campaign worker for a fictional presidential candidate. Jodie Foster portrayed Iris, a young prostitute.

Bob suspected that certain story elements were influenced by Arthur H. Bremer's journal, *An Assassin's Diary*. Entries in the diary cover the approximately six weeks leading up to Bremer's 1972 assassination attempt on George Wallace. Bremer had originally stalked President Richard Nixon. Unable to find a surefire opportunity to assassinate the president, Bremer switched to an alternate target, Governor Wallace. Bremer had also considered shooting Secret Service agents en masse.

Looking for clues to detect would-be assassins, Bob had studied Bremer's life and diary in detail. Bob saw similarities between the character Bickle and the real-life Bremer, and it wasn't just that both last names started with a "B" and contained six letters. Travis Bickle hails from the Midwest. He's a loner with serious emotional issues. Bickle does not have satisfying relationships with females and cannot achieve sexual fulfillment. He endures severe headaches. After rejection, Bickle feels he has to do something "big." He buys weapons, stalks a presidential candidate, and engages in a dangerous game of cat and mouse with the Secret Service. Both stories end in violence.

Concerned with the copycat phenomenon, Bob was afraid some vulnerable misfit would identify with the Travis Bickle character. "This country has plenty of alienated ne'er-do-wells who are anti-social and anti-authority," Bob warned. "Troubled, impressionable minds might try to emulate what they see in *Taxi Driver*. The film presents a violent prescription for those who would want to shock society into noticing them. Through cold-blooded murder, the lead character gains fame and *even* receives some exoneration," Bob said in a tone of disgust. "They turned a suicidal sociopath into a hero."

"Bobbie, it's just a movie," I replied.

"To you and me and most everyone else, it's just a movie. To a few, it might be the fantasy to kill and to die for," cautioned Bob.

Back in the field office, Bob worked an especially memorable case with PI Squad Agent Dick Corrigan. The subject sent a rambling letter to the secretary of the treasury with language that could be construed as a veiled threat. The subject had been accused by the Securities and Exchange Commission (SEC) of defrauding $200,000 from investors. Subject's attorney agreed to present his client for an interview by the Secret Service as long as the subject was not asked about the pending SEC case.

Even though the attorney was present and had advised the subject to answer the questions, the individual was uncooperative and verbally combative. After naming some politicians and others he didn't like and ranting about what was wrong with America, the subject stormed out of the attorney's office. Dick stayed to talk with the attorney, while Bob followed the subject outside. Bob observed that the individual was walking with a limp. "How did you hurt your leg?" Bob asked.

"In a parachute jump," answered the subject.

"Were you in the military?"

"I went to a civilian jump school," the subject replied angrily.

"Look, we don't want to add to your troubles. We're just trying to resolve the matter of this one letter," Bob remarked.

"I don't want to talk about it," the subject stated emphatically as he reached his car door.

Using a different tack, Bob quickly asked, "Who do you like?"

The individual immediately answered, "Gary Cooper, now there's a *real* American hero." With that, the subject jumped behind the wheel, started his car, and drove out of the parking lot.

Later, Dick and Bob interviewed the subject's wife and found her to be elusive too. She was prone to break down in tears. Bob had the feeling that she was hiding something. Bob also noticed men's adventure magazines on the coffee table at the couple's residence.

In the days that followed, Corrigan was informed by the subject's attorney that his client did not want to be further interviewed by the Secret Service. The attorney also remarked that the subject was upset that his wife had been questioned by Dick and Bob.

Next, the individual sent another letter to the secretary of the treasury. This time, the subject threatened some form of retaliation if either he or his wife were contacted again by agents of the Treasury Department. With this turn of events, Dick and Bob gathered to discuss the case. Dick's preliminary evaluation had been that the subject did not present a danger to Secret Service protectees. "What do you think, Bob?" Dick asked.

"I think this guy is of protective interest. He's a hot head, who doesn't like his country. He's been accused of some serious criminal activity. He's writing letters with conditional threats. His emotional state is deteriorating. The world is closing in on him. In his desperation, he might resort to some sort of senseless act that would incorporate violence."

"Bob, I have the feeling he's just a lot of talk. Do you think he presents a danger to the secretary?"

"He certainly has a direction of interest toward the secretary."

"Do you think he's for real?" Dick asked.

"Yes, I think he's capable of reckless, dangerous behavior."

"Okay, there's no need to take chances. We'll go with your instincts. I'll write him up as being of protective interest for the time being."

Several weeks later, Dick received some alarming news from the U.S. Attorney's Office. The subject had just been arrested by the FBI for extortion. He was charged with attempting to extort a large sum of money from an interstate bus company. It was alleged that the subject had threatened to blow up some of the buses of the company unless a payment was made. It was believed that the subject had sent a package containing explosives to the bus line. The parcel exploded in a Washington, D.C. post office before it could be delivered. Fortunately, no one was hurt.

The news was an affirmation of Bob's evaluation. Hearing Dick relating the recent events brought to Bob's mind one of the most famous cases in the annals of crime. "Sit down, Dick, and let me run something by you," Bob burst out excitedly. "This might sound a bit farfetched, but I've been troubled about our guy for some time."

As he took a seat, Dick interjected: "I'm a believer. Lay it on me, my brother."

"Dick, remember the FBI circular regarding D.B. Cooper?"

"Yeah, the Feebies [FBI] sent some information about the sky-jacking to law enforcement agencies in hope Cooper could be identified."

"I looked over the circular pretty thoroughly," Bob stated. "I think you should write up our man and submit him to the FBI; they might want to take a look at him in the Cooper case."

"Tell me why you think so," Dick mused—intrigued by what he had just heard.

"About four years ago on Thanksgiving eve 1971, a white male purchased a ticket for a Northwest Orient Airlines flight from Portland to Seattle," Bob began. "D.B. Cooper is a misnomer that the press got hold of early in the investigation, and it stuck with the public. According to the FBI, the hijacker actually used the name *Dan Cooper* when purchasing his ticket."

"Bob, you're kidding me. Why didn't the Bureau correct the mistake?"

"Maybe they wanted an easy way to weed out hoaxers," Bob speculated. "In any case, our guy's name is *Dan*. It's worth mentioning that his given name is Dan, not Daniel.

"And when I followed him from the attorney's office," Bob continued, "I noticed he walked with a limp. He told me he injured his leg in a parachute jump. Since he had told us plenty of things and people he didn't like, I tried the other side of the coin. I asked him whom he did like. Without hesitation, he answered, 'Gary Cooper.' I didn't think much about it at the time."

"The movie star Gary Cooper," Dick intimated.

"I can only assume so because our guy referred to Cooper as a 'real American hero.' Gary Cooper was an action film hero. With our subject's recent caper, his answers could take on new meaning. If you take our guy's first name and Gary Cooper's last name, you might have an alter ego, *Dan Cooper*. I saw men's adventure magazines at our subject's residence, like *Argosy* and *True*. This guy might be living out his fantasies.

"Taking this further, the $200,000 Cooper extorted from Northwest Airlines is the *same* amount our subject is accused of swindling," Bob added. "And our guy just got arrested for trying to extort money from an interstate transportation company with threats to blow up their vehicles. That's a similar MO [modus operandi]."

"Bob—on that point—why would our man risk doing something like that now?"

"He was probably trying to score some quick cash to flee the country. He's becoming more desperate, and he's looking for a way out."

"You're probably right."

"Bob, the circumstantial evidence you presented is more than enough to justify alerting the FBI. I'll write it up and send it to Liaison for forwarding to the Bureau."

At the end of January 1976, further validation of our boys' evaluation surfaced. The subject attempted suicide before his court date by taking an overdose of sleeping pills. Bob came home that night and told me how he and Corrigan were being praised for their accurate assessment of the subject. He had certainly proven to be dangerous.

Several weeks passed; Dick and Bob's subject had one more trick up his sleeve. He escaped from the custody of U.S. marshals while being transported between the federal courthouse and jail. Although Bob received a tip that the subject was hiding out in Greenwich Village, New York, the FBI believed the subject had fled to Canada. In any case, the FBI and Marshals Service had primary jurisdiction over the subject. Bob, Dick, and the rest of the agents in the PI squad had plenty of other subjects, visits, movements, and events to worry about.

Bob had a special knack for handling PI subjects, especially those who wished to speak to the president in person. When making contact with subjects exhibiting abnormal or disturbed behavior, Bob first assessed whether the subject presented an *immediate* danger. Bob listened to the subject for verbal clues and closely watched his or her hands and demeanor. Looking for bulges and other signs of concealed weapons, Bob would frisk the subject if conditions warranted.

Next, Bob attempted to establish rapport. Intently listening to the statements made by subjects, Bob showed concern for their plight. Many PI subjects felt frustrated, and they were seeking relief from problems that overwhelmed them. Although these problems might be imaginary and the subjects' concerns unfounded, they were all too real to individuals with psychotic disorders (out of touch with reality). Outwardly disagreeing with demented individuals or trivializing their concerns could provoke anger and violent behavior. As Bob said, "It does little good to try and reason with an irrational mind."

Utilizing strategies during the interview that did *not* incorporate obvious pretext, Bob got the subjects to provide the needed identifying and personal history information. It was important that agents did not lie to mental subjects, even if it succeeded in getting the subjects to comply with a resented course of action. Once subjects realized they had been deceived, they could feel threatened and become uncooperative and even violent.

Some PI subjects continued to come to the attention of the Secret Service on repeat occasions. It would be that more difficult to handle the subject the next time if he or she felt betrayed. It was essential that PI subjects held positive thoughts toward the president and the Secret Service. Otherwise, subjects might turn their fear and suspicion to the president or USSS agents and resort to offensive actions.

Bob was particularly successful in diverting subjects from their attempts to talk with the president. Even though the subjects did not accomplish their mission to have an audience with the president, Bob made them feel that they had achieved the essential part of their goal. For example, Bob assured subjects who were not a danger that the information would be presented to higher authorities and that all appropriate action would be taken. Thus, subjects could return home knowing they had done everything that was necessary and possible.

Bob would then notify the subject's family for assistance in making travel arrangements. Bob put many a PI subject on a bus back to their hometown. With these subjects, the main goal was to get them out of Washington, so they wouldn't be tempted to return to the White House.

With subjects that were being referred to St. Elizabeths Hospital (*no* apostrophe) for psychological evaluation, Bob advised that the first step in the process of getting this information to higher authorities was that the information had to be verified and evaluated. The subject would have to be seen by a person who specialized in these matters.

Of the mentally ill subjects who had a direction of interest to the president, Bob found that their discourse fell into two broad categories. In the first, subjects believed they had the solution for some pressing world problem, or they wanted to warn of some impending catastrophe or apocalyptic event. These ranged from irrational ways to solve issues such as world hunger to dire warnings of a sneak attack by the Soviets or by aliens from outer space, etc.

In the second category, subjects complained of imaginary ailments and accused others of causing them harm. Often, subjects complained that their homes were bugged and that they were being spied on. In severe cases, government agencies were blamed for bombarding the subjects with radar waves and the like for mind control. Subjects wanted the president to order the responsible parties to stop these intrusions. It was not uncommon for subjects to place aluminum foil inside their hats or clothes to ward off the imaginary rays.

The latter exhibited paranoid schizophrenia and the most dangerous ones were those who heard voices ordering the elimination of something or someone for the good of society. Command hallucinations coupled with persecutory delusions could be a lethal mix.

Next to paranoid schizophrenia, the most common psychosis medically diagnosed for PI subjects was manic depression. Commonly called bipolar disorder today, subjects generally came to the attention of the Secret Service during the manic phase of the illness. These episodes were characterized by overactive behavior—both physical and mental. Racing thoughts, poor judgment, rapid speech, impulsiveness, overestimation of true abilities, arrogance, exaggerated sense of well-being, restlessness, and insomnia were some of the symptoms.

The delusions of bipolar subjects in manic episodes normally focus on grandeur. In this exalted state, subjects could quickly become irritated, angry, and violent when their activities were blocked by authority figures. Frenzied thoughts and behavior could produce elevated strength and stubborn resistance.

On one occasion, it took Bob and two police officers five minutes to subdue a bipolar subject and to get him safely into the transport wagon. This was an especially dangerous operation. The subject had to be taken into custody at his residence. A law enforcement officer never knows where the subject might have a weapon hidden. Plus, there's always the danger that the subject might be able to wrestle a handgun away from an agent or officer. Until one can get handcuffs on a subject who is resisting arrest—especially a charged-up mental subject—lives can be in jeopardy.

Chapter 7

Descent into Darkness

In September 1976, Bob was asked if he would like an over-seas TDY (temporary duty) assignment with the USSS pro-tective detail for Secretary of State Henry Kissinger. Bob didn't particularly want the travel but thought it would be fun to work again with some of his old friends.

Plus, Bob would be protecting Kissinger as he embarked on an important diplomatic mission to Europe and Africa. Kissinger would consult with foreign leaders on the worsening racial strife in South-West Africa (Namibia) and Rhodesia (Zimbabwe). There was serious concern that full-scale war with Cold War overtones would erupt in the region. Due to the need for height-ened security and the number of agents out on advances, the Kissinger Detail supplemented its working shifts with agents from the field.

Bob's shift was directed to fly ahead via USAF transport to Lu-saka, Zambia—one of Kissinger's first African stops. For these airlifts, C-141A transport planes were utilized. The Lockheed C-141A Starlifters were four-engine jet aircraft, which could cruise at over 500 miles per hour. The planes featured clamshell rear doors and a loading ramp. A good portion of the 145-foot length of the aircraft was devoted to cargo area. Even with two vehicles in the cargo compartment, there was room to install rows of aft-facing seats for passengers. That's how the "car plane," as USSS agents called it, was configured for Air Force special air mis-sions (SAMs) in support of the Secret Service.

For this trip, the car plane was loaded with an armored lim-ousine and a station wagon follow-up. The vehicles were se-cured to the deck with sturdy steel chains. To assure a reliable supply of fuel, drums of high-octane gasoline were strapped along the sides of the cargo area along with other security gear and personal luggage.

The C-141 headed south from Europe toward the African continent. It was estimated to be about a nine-hour flight. Diplomatic clearances had been requested from nations the C-141 would flyover. One African country did not respond in time. The C-141 had to be vectored around that nation's territory. This added extra time to the flight, but more importantly the aircraft consumed a greater amount of fuel.

It was early morning when the C-141 approached Lusaka International Airport—about 35 minutes till sunrise. To the shock of the aircraft's crew, the airport was dark. The runway lights were off and there were no navigational aids operating. The flight crew rechecked their directory of international airports and confirmed that the listing for Lusaka International showed it was operational 24 hours a day.

Attempts to raise the airport's control tower via radio were unsuccessful. Finally, a voice responded—presumably in the Zambian language of Nyanja. The pilot asked for someone to come to the mike who could speak English. Several minutes later, an English-speaking voice broke over the radio, "This is Lusaka, go ahead." The pilot informed the ground party of the flight specifics and that the military attaché at the U.S. Embassy had passed all to the Zambian government and appropriate permissions had been granted. The pilot emphasized in no uncertain terms that the approach and runway lights needed to come on immediately, as the C-141 was low on fuel. The reply from the airport was unnerving: "Airport operations won't commence until later this morning. There are no scheduled flights for hours."

"Lusaka, get your lights operational. We have proper diplomatic clearance and need to land now!" boomed the C-141 pilot.

"There's no one here but the cleaning crew. I'm speaking with you from the radio set in the maintenance office," replied the voice on the radio.

"Roger, Lusaka. Get whatever airport lights on you can. Then line up all the vehicles available along the sides of the runway, so their headlights can shine on the tarmac. Be as quick as you can because this bird is coming down in two-zero minutes—one way or another."

"WILCO [will comply]," came the reply from the ground.

The loadmaster of the C-141 scrambled around the compartment, double-checking that the cargo was secured and that all of the agents were belted tightly in their seats. Agents were briefed on bracing techniques and other rough-landing procedures.

Along with several other agents, who were in the first row of seats, Bob sat directly in front of the black Cadillac armored limo. The cargo compartment of the C-141 was 10 feet wide. The limo filled Bob's peripheral vision like a 12,000-pound monster. "This must be the last thing someone sees when they're run over by a Cadillac," Bob joked to those around him. Bob's head was about hood high with his legs only inches from the bumper of the black behemoth—close enough to reach out and touch the license plate.

The loadmaster informed the agents that the aircraft would circle as long as possible to allow ground personnel time to illuminate the field and for the approaching sunrise. With the flight engineer closely monitoring the gauges, the minutes ticked away, while the pounds of fuel in the tanks dropped to the minimum required for safety. The aircraft commander announced that he was bringing the plane in.

The sun was just rising along the eastern horizon. The aircraft quickly descended, and without warning the landing gear forcibly collided with the runway. The shock wave of touchdown energy penetrated through Bob's back like a jackhammer.

Suddenly coming to life, the massive Cadillac sprung from the cargo deck. The steel chain links tightened and strained to their limits. For a couple of rapid heartbeats, Bob feared the chains might break, savagely unleashing 12,000 pounds of steel. Just as rapidly as the Cadillac had risen, it thundered back down to the deck with a roar and shuddered considerably. "This is the roughest landing I've ever seen," yelled the agent next to Bob. "I thought we crashed!"

The muscle spasms that immediately flared in Bob's back proved the point. Bob felt the heightened pain. Bob's lower back pain had never completely gone away since the time he was rear ended during his Park Police days. His back was further aggravated during a State Department counterterrorist driving school. The practical exercises consisted of actual vehicle ramming and the like.

The vehicles were offloaded along with the other USSS equipment and personal luggage, and the shift checked into the Intercontinental Hotel Lusaka. Agents were posted to four-hour shifts to guard the limo and follow-up, which were being kept in the hotel's parking lot. When not safeguarding the vehicles, the agents were free to catch up on sleep or to do some sightseeing.

The next day, USSS shift leader Ken Clark held a meeting in his hotel room. He had just arrived back from the American Embassy with the latest news. "Do you want the bad news or the *really* bad news first?" Clark asked his agents.

One of the agents piped up, "Don't we have any good news?"

The furrows in Clark's forehead rippled with tension. "No," Clark answered tersely. After a brief pause, Clark began: "The bad news is there's intelligence that rebel forces might try to hijack the armored limo and follow-up. I'm going to double-up our security coverage. From now on, two agents will be assigned to each four-hour shift. I want you to take all of the shoulder weapons out of the follow-up and store them with you in the armored limo. If anything should happen, get the word out over the radio and drive the limo to the American Embassy. The rest of us will meet you there."

"Ken, there's a truck load of Zambian troops in the parking lot and sentries around the hotel. The embassy in Lusaka doesn't seem to be that secure. It's right off the street with only one local guard out front and a Marine inside. Wouldn't we be safer at the hotel if something goes down?" one of the agents asked.

"That brings me to the *really* bad news," Clark replied. "When black African leaders became aware of the secretary's meeting with the South African prime minister in Zurich, they decided to hold their own summit in Tanzania. Guerilla leaders were included in the meetings as well as the presidents of Mozambique and Angola. They're backed by the Soviet Union and Cuba. It's believed the revolutionaries and their supporters want to tie the problem of South African apartheid [official policy of segregation] with the other issues. That would be a deal breaker with the South Africans and kill any chance for peace. Dr. K. decided the time isn't right to begin mediation in Africa. He's returning to Washington to consult with President Ford and to see what plays out. The trip to Lusaka has been postponed for at least a week."

Groans and moans broke out from the assembled agents. Some expletives were uttered. "Listen up," Clark ordered. "There's more. The car plane left early this morning. A tire and possibly the nose gear were damaged during the landing. It's flying to a base in Europe to be checked and repaired. It will return, but for the time being we're stranded. Since Dr. Kissinger postponed his trip, the Zambians pulled the plug on the troops at the hotel. We're on our own and in a region that might break out in war at any moment." More expletives were spoken.

In Lusaka, Bob and the other agents guarded the cars 24 x 7. To keep the batteries charged and to run routes, the vehicles were driven around Lusaka in a two-car motorcade on several occasions. Zambians watched in wonder as the big, black Caddy and black Mercury station wagon—both sporting Washington, D.C. tags—cruised around the streets of the city. A fun part of one of the outings was when the motorcade stopped at a local playground. The children flocked to the cars for a peek inside and to get some bubblegum and candy bars from the agents.

The word from Tanzania was that President Nyerere was not optimistic about the chances for peace. The Africans wanted black-majority rule now *and* an end to apartheid. Otherwise, there were threats "to fight to the last man." President Nyerere did agree, however, that Kissinger should continue on his mission.

Secretary Kissinger arrived in Lusaka where he conferred with Zambian President Kenneth Kaunda. Bob stood in the halls of the Zambian State House, which resembles a small-scale White House, while Kissinger sought acceptance for the British-American plan. Kaunda, a moderate on black-white issues, advised the U.S. secretary of state that time was running out. Kaunda warned that Southern Africa was only days—not weeks—away from an escalation to full-scale warfare.

After several days of negotiation, Kaunda gave his blessing to Secretary Kissinger to travel to Pretoria, South Africa. Kaunda felt this was the last chance for peace and that overruled his aversion of giving any recognition to the white-minority regime in Pretoria.

In Pretoria, Kissinger negotiated with Prime Minister John Vorster, listened to the concerns of South African black leaders, and ultimately met with Rhodesian prime minister Ian Smith.

In the meantime, Bob's shift flew via car plane to Kinshasa, Zaire to prepare for the secretary's upcoming visit with Zairian President Mobutu Sese Seko. Kinshasa (formerly Leopoldville, Belgian Congo) sits within the Zaire River basin and receives over 50 inches of rain a year. Hit with a one-two punch of high temperature and oppressive humidity, Bob sweltered in the stifling mist of a tropical rain forest.

Secretary Kissinger arrived in Kinshasa with high hopes. He had received indications from both Vorster and Smith that they favored the proposed peace plan over warfare. Adding the positive reactions of presidents Nyerere and Kaunda, the prospect of moving toward nonviolent resolutions of Southern African racial problems looked much better. President Mobutu received the good news with relief. Pleased with Kissinger's progress, Mobutu—in an unexpected move—invited the secretary for a dinner cruise on the Zaire River (also known as the Congo River).

One of the longest rivers in the world, the Zaire runs almost 3,000 miles and has depths over 500 feet. The river was the setting for Joseph Conrad's 1902 novel *Heart of Darkness*. In 1976, river steamers still plied the Zaire between Kinshasa and Kisangani (formerly Stanleyville). When word reached the Secret Service command post that Kissinger had accepted Mobutu's impromptu invitation, Ken Clark announced to his agents with much concern: "Great, now we've got to do a last-minute advance of a steamboat. Does *anyone* know *anything* about steamboats?"

Clark was surprised when Bob volunteered the following: "Ken, I don't know about steamboats as such, but I did have instruction on boilers when I was a county housing inspector, before starting my law enforcement career. Many of the apartment buildings have some pretty big ones."

Clark looked at Bob with some amazement: "You're with me. We'll grab the EOD man and get Nkulu [Zairian official who was the USSS advance contact] to run us over there. The secretary and Mobutu will depart in a couple of hours."

A short time later, the men pulled up to a small pathway that led from the road to the bank of the Zaire River. The path was about three feet wide and cut a swath through the dense vegetation, which covered the riverside. As the advance party stepped down the trail, Clark caught sight of some men moving around in the underbrush. "Nkulu," Clark said, "who are those men? We have to get them out of there—for security reasons."

Nkulu looked at Clark without expression and responded in a matter-of-fact way, "They are catching killer snakes, so Mr. Kissinger does not get bitten and die." Just then, one of the bushmen lifted up a pole with a three-foot serpentine shape clinging to it. He deftly dropped his catch into a large burlap bag and continued to pole through the brush. Three sets of American eyes quickly scanned the trail, as Ken, Bob, and Rich, the EOD man, suddenly realized that street shoes and a business suit don't offer much protection against the razor-sharp fangs of venomous snakes.

"Nkulu, those men may stay there!" Clark affirmed loudly. "What types of poisonous snakes are found here?"

"Mambas and vipers," answered Nkulu. "If you are bitten, you have no more than one-half hour to reach hospital for anti-venin."

The party quickly moved to the riverbank where a gangplank had been dropped from the steamer, an aging stern-wheeler. A relic from a by-gone era of European colonialism, the ship now reflected the stark reality of third-world economics. Her white paint was grimy from years of equatorial service and lack of upkeep. Smoke belched from rusted smokestacks as the lady was being readied for yet one more run.

"Bob, do a safety inspection of the engine room," directed Clark. "Rich, start your EOD sweep. Nkulu and I will head for the wheelhouse where we'll coordinate with the captain. I don't see any lifeboats. I've got a lot of questions."

Bob went below deck to the engine room. What he found was a scene that could have come out of *The African Queen*—the 1951 action-adventure film, which starred Humphrey Bogart and Katharine Hepburn. The story was based on the 1935 novel by C.S. Forester and set along a dangerous stretch of the Congo in war torn 1914. The engine room Bob entered more resembled that earlier period than present day. Everything in it looked original. The boiler was an old, hand-riveted one. Steam escaped from loose-fitting rivets and from pipes connected to the boiler. The water in the boiler was heated by wood.

The ship's engineer was an elderly gentleman. He stood by watching pressure gauges as a young assistant threw wood into the firebox to get up steam. Bob nodded to the engineer and moved alongside of him. The gauges were old and worn. Most troubling, the main safety gauge was not operating properly. Its needle fluctuated wildly between low and high-pressure readings. It would be impossible to obtain an accurate reading to warn of dangerous redline pressure buildup.

As the boiler moaned and groaned, Bob checked it for cracks and signs of stress. He inspected the leaking pipe joints, literally bandaged with cloth bindings. There were no certificates of inspection or maintenance records to be found. No safety equipment could be seen. To sum it up, the engine room was an inspector's *worst* nightmare.

Bob moved to the wheelhouse where Ken—with Nkulu interpreting—was not finding the captain very receptive to USSS inquiries. Needing a breather, Ken motioned Bob to the outside deck. "How did it go?" Clark asked.

"Ken, this boat's a relic. It's probably been decades since anyone opened up the boiler and inspected it. I didn't see any signs of maintenance. The main pressure gauge is shot. We've got leaks from rivets and pipes. There's rust everywhere."

"That bad, huh?"

"Yep."

"Okay, Bob, help out Rich with the EOD sweep. I'll stay here with Nkulu and see what I can learn from the captain. It looks like this tug doesn't have radar or much in the way of emergency equipment."

Bob found Rich on the main deck, watching three Zairians in a rowboat. Well, only two of them were actually in the boat. The other was in the water. He was being held underwater by the ankles while the third man paddled the craft along the side of the steamboat. "Rich, what are those guys doing?" Bob asked a bit bewildered.

Portraying a *now I've seen everything* look, Rich answered, "I *think* they're checking the hull for explosives."

Bob assisted Rich in finishing the EOD sweep, and the two men met up with Clark and Nkulu in the ship's dining room. "I'm worried about the hull inspection," Rich stated to Nkulu. "We need divers to check under the boat."

"Crocodiles may be nearby," Nkulu replied. "Better to stay in dinghy."

"Nkulu, besides poisonous snakes and crocodiles, what other dangers are there?" Clark asked.

"Upriver, there are cannibals. But we won't be going that far."

"Good, let's stay well clear of the cannibals," Clark emphasized. "Will we have escort craft from the military with us on the cruise?"

"We should have a patrol boat join us," Nkulu answered.

"Nkulu, will you please check in the galley to see what is being prepared for Dr. Kissinger. Later, I'll need to randomly select the actual meal and beverage that will be offered," Clark advised.

After Nkulu left the table, Clark asked Rich about the EOD sweep. "A local looked under the hull. I can't guarantee that it's clean. I did the best I could in my sweep. Without a dog, divers, and more time, something could still be planted."

"Guys, I'm recommending the secretary passes on this stop," Clark announced. "We've got too many potential dangers here. We'd need days to make this safe." Clark then radioed the detail leader and advised him of the particulars. In spite of Clark's warning, Secretary Kissinger decided to continue on the outing. The cruise was mercifully cut short, however, when Kissinger was called back to the U.S. Embassy for some important cable traffic regarding other global issues. Although the problems of Southern Africa were paramount at the time, Secretary Kissinger had to be concerned with other hot spots and diplomatic problems around the world.

After Zaire, Dr. Kissinger traveled to Nairobi, Kenya where he consulted with President Jomo Kenyatta. Kissinger ended this round of "shuttle diplomacy" for discussion in London with British Foreign Secretary Anthony Crosland.

Back at WFO, one PI investigation is remembered for its peculiarity and uniqueness. It began one Saturday afternoon when the USSS Intelligence Division duty desk supervisor called Bob at home. An incident had just occurred at Andrews Air Force Base. Although Bob was not the PI Squad duty agent that weekend, he was being called because we lived close to Andrews.

The pilot of a private aircraft with two other persons on board had declared an emergency and had landed at AAFB. Once on the ground, the pilot stated he was a CIA operative with highly sensitive national security information. The intelligence needed to be *immediately* delivered to the White House Situation Room.

Inside the terminal building, the subject ordered up an Air Force staff car for the drive to the White House. By now, the deputy base commander had been called to the scene. The colonel talked briefly with the subject and believed him to be genuine. While a car was being readied, the colonel called the White House to advise them of the emergency. Eventually, USSS-ID received the call. They asked the colonel to keep the subject at Andrews until an agent could respond. The colonel agreed but warned that the subject claimed to have time-sensitive compartmented information. The subject was quoted as saying, "Many lives are in jeopardy."

Bob grabbed his gear and ran out of the house to the government car. After expediting to Andrews with lights and siren, Bob arrived at the passenger terminal where he checked in with the deputy base commander and his chief of security police, an Air Force captain. "Where's the subject?" Bob asked.

"All three subjects are inside this office," replied the captain as he pointed to a nearby door.

"Let's put them in separate rooms. I'd like to talk to each of them individually. Have they been patted down for weapons?" Bob asked.

"No, sir," answered the captain. "I do have driver permits for all three."

"Has the aircraft been checked for explosives?"

"Negative," said the captain—looking a bit uneasy.

"Under the circumstances, can we get a dog to sniff out the aircraft?" Bob requested.

"Certainly," replied the captain, who then called his control center via a portable radio and relayed the request.

Next, the three subjects were separated into different rooms. Two of the men were in their 40s while the remaining man was 19 years old. Bob ran the subjects through ID and NCIC (National Crime Information Computer) with no record found. The plane's tail number was checked through NCIC. There were no wants.

"I'll start with the teenager first," Bob advised.

"May I sit in on the interview?" asked the colonel.

"Of course," Bob replied.

Bob entered the room followed by the colonel. Bob pulled a chair over to the desk where subject number three was sitting. After identifying himself, Bob informed the subject, "I want to advise you that under federal law you're an adult, so there's no misunderstanding." Bob then followed up with the Miranda warning. Afterwards, subject number three signed a waiver, stating he wanted to talk with Bob and without an attorney present.

"Do you have any weapons, explosives, or contraband on you or in the plane?" Bob began.

"No, sir!" replied the subject—shaking his head a couple of times for emphasis.

"Okay, give me the short version as to how you got to be here today."

"I was at the Mercer County Airport this morning. That's near Trenton, New Jersey. I'm taking lessons to get my private pilot's license. My instructor, Mr. Davis, came to me and offered me a chance to get some extra flying time. A man was renting a plane for a trip to Washington. Mr. Davis would be going along. He asked if I wanted to go too and fly the plane back."

"Who flew the plane down here?" asked Bob.

"The guy who rented the plane," answered the subject. "I don't know his name. He didn't talk much."

"What happened when you got into the Washington area?"

"We flew around for a while. Mr. Davis didn't know what was going on. He asked the man what airport we would be landing at. The guy mumbled something about the White House. Then he gets on the radio and declares an emergency. Mr. Davis asked what was going on. The man said he had to get to the White House. Then, he lands us at an Air Force base."

Next, Bob interviewed Mr. Davis, subject number two. He gave the same story with a bit more detail. Davis was the operator of a flying service. Subject number one showed up this morning wanting to rent an aircraft. The subject had a current pilot's license and a valid credit card. Davis rented him a plane.

Davis got worried when he observed the individual over revving the engine and making other errors on the taxiway. The subject appeared to be out of practice and was not cleared for takeoff.

After subject number one said he needed to get to Washington in a hurry, Davis offered to accompany him in order to ensure the safe and proper operation of the aircraft—and its return. Davis invited a student pilot along, so he could get some flight time too.

Once in the Washington air corridor, subject said he needed to get to the White House. After flying around for a while, subject number one finally saw the runways at Andrews AFB. Davis was speechless when the subject radioed the tower at AAFB and declared an emergency.

Bob and the colonel then moved to door number one. The subject claiming to be a CIA operative had a New Jersey driver's license in the name of Arturo Gonzales. Bob showed his credentials and White House pass to the subject. After advising Gonzales of his Miranda rights and receiving a signed waiver, Bob started the questioning. "Tell me why you have to get to the White House."

"I can't divulge that to you," the subject stated in a Spanish accent. "This is highly sensitive information. I've been involved in a CIA operation and barely escaped with my life. This is urgent national security information that needs to be personally relayed to the duty officer at the White House Situation Room—*immediately*. The longer you keep me here with these games, the more likely many people are going to die!"

"Then you better tell me what it is," Bob stated authoritatively. "I have top-secret clearance with unqualified SI access. The colonel is fully cleared too. You made an emergency landing at a restricted military installation. You're representing yourself as a government agent, who has official business at the White House. Until you satisfy us, you aren't going anywhere."

"Okay," said the subject, "you win. But what I say stays in this room. This morning, I escaped from Russian agents. They were holding me captive—somewhere in New Jersey. The Soviet Union has developed a top-secret device that they plan to activate tomorrow at 2:00 p.m. sharp. This machine will send the Moon into a collision course with the Earth. They have it set, so the Moon will strike only the United States and wipe us out. I must get this information to the White House Situation Room! It means life or death for all of us!"

Bob rose from his chair and opened the door to the corridor where the AF security police captain was standing. "You can cancel the staff car. Order up Mr. Wheels [police transport] for our man instead," Bob advised. "He'll be visiting St. E's first."

Bob then obtained the subject's background and filled out the referral papers for the hospital. Since Andrews was a federal installation within the "environs of the District of Columbia," Bob could refer the subject directly to St. Elizabeths. Bob finished the interview by taking some mug shots with a Kodak Instamatic camera. All PI agents carried them in the field.

The two other men received a stern warning from the colonel and Bob—especially to be more cautious about whom they ride with in an airplane. They were released and allowed to return in the aircraft to New Jersey.

Bob called ID and notified them of the outcome. Then he packed up his paperwork and rose to say goodbye to the deputy base commander. The colonel extended a hand in gratitude: "Thanks, I can't believe I almost sent that guy to the White House in an official vehicle. You saved my career. If there is anything, I can *ever* do for you—short of treason—let me know."

Chapter 8
1977

March 1977 was quite an unusual month for the Secret Service—especially for the agents in Washington. Wednesday, March 9, 1977, is better remembered for the acts of terrorism that took our nation's capital by surprise.

At about 11:00 a.m. that morning, seven men stormed into the B'nai B'rith (Jewish service organization) building at 1640 Rhode Island Avenue, NW, D.C. Wielding guns and machetes and searching floor by floor, the intruders rounded up over a hundred people and forced them into an eighth-floor conference room. There, the captors bound their hostages and forced them to lie face down on the floor. The windows of the conference room were painted over to cut off the view from the outside.

About an hour later, three armed men entered the Islamic Center at 2551 Massachusetts Avenue, NW, in the heart of Embassy Row. Twelve hostages were seized. The abductors tied up their captives and held them at gunpoint. Hostages had now been taken at two D.C. locations.

While this was going on, Bob and a handful of other agents were on their way to the headquarters building of the Central Intelligence Agency, located in Langley, Virginia (a short drive from D.C.). The agents were assigned to provide protective support for President Carter's visit to the CIA.

The president participated in the swearing-in ceremony of Admiral Stansfield Turner as the new Director of the CIA. The president then addressed the approximately 450 persons in attendance.

With the president's 2:49 p.m. departure from CIA Headquarters, Bob and the other agents were released to return to Washington. During the drive back, Bob was called on the radio and ordered to respond to the District Building (renamed John A. Wilson Building in 1994) located at 1350 Pennsylvania Avenue, NW, D.C. Apparently, a shooting had just occurred at that location. Bob was dispatched to the scene to monitor the situation. The building was *only* a couple of blocks from the White House.

Bob checked in at the police command post, which had been hastily set up in a room on the fourth floor of the District Building. One floor above, two men were holding 13 persons captive within the offices of the D.C. City Council. One of the men was armed with a shotgun; the other brandished a machete.

During the initial takeover, two shotgun blasts were fired at security officers. One of the officers was wounded, while a bystander, WHUR-FM news reporter Maurice Williams, was killed.

Shots broke out again a few moments later when city police arrived on the scene. During this exchange, the gunman shot a hostage, who was lying face down on the floor. It was a warning to police that innocent lives were in danger. Hearing the terrified cries of hostages, police held their fire and a standoff ensued.

With the seizure at the District Building, well over a hundred hostages were being held at *three* separate D.C. locations. Fear and panic were spreading throughout the city. Security was tightened in government buildings. Fearing additional takeovers, officials closed the Municipal Building (300 Indiana Avenue, NW) as well as the Washington Monument and Lincoln and Jefferson Memorials.

Bob learned that all three incidents were connected. The hostage takers were members of the Hanafi Moslems, a small religious sect, whose members were mostly black Americans. The organization had its headquarters in a house at 7700 16th Street, NW, D.C. The home was purchased for the group by then Milwaukee Bucks basketball star Kareem Abdul-Jabbar, who was a member of the sect. The founder and leader of the order, Hamaas Abdul Khaalis, was one of the seven men who were now holding hostages at the B'nai B'rith building.

Khaalis had been a former member and official in the Nation of Islam (NOI). He left that organization in 1958 over religious differences. Khaalis moved to Washington and formed his own order in the mid-1960s. In 1972, Hamaas Abdul Khaalis sent an open letter critical of NOI leader Elijah Muhammad to a number of Black Muslim mosques.

In January 1973, seven members of the Hanafi were brutally murdered in their 16th Street home. All were relatives of Khaalis. It was the largest mass murder in Washington history.

Eight men from the Philadelphia area with ties to the Black Muslim community were charged with the murders. Prosecutors argued that the killings were retribution for the inflammatory letters authored by Khaalis.

Five of the eight were eventually convicted of murder. Four were serving lengthy prison sentences while the remaining subject had his conviction overturned. He was awaiting a new trial.

Hamaas Abdul Khaalis believed the murders of his family had been executions ordered by certain Black Muslim leaders. He was critical of police and government officials for not pursuing these allegations. In addition, Khaalis was upset that those convicted of the murders had not been executed.

Now, Khaalis and his followers had taken matters in their own hands. Khaalis wanted to extract his own justice under the principles of Islamic law. Early on during negotiations with D.C. Police Chief Maurice Cullinane and Deputy Chief Robert Rabe, Hamaas Abdul Khaalis demanded that the murderers of his children and of Malcolm X be handed over to the Hanafis. It soon became clear why some of Khaalis' men carried machetes. Khaalis was engaged in a jihad (holy war) and wanted blood for blood. If the killers were not delivered to him, Khaalis threatened to behead hostages.

Supported by specialists from the Department of Justice, State Department, and the Behavioral Science Unit (BSU) of the FBI, Cullinane and Rabe attempted to establish trust and rapport with Khaalis. The MPD officials wanted to set in motion a negotiation process that would preclude the setting of ultimatums and deadlines and eventually lead to a peaceful resolution of the crisis.

Cullinane and Rabe were also aided by the ambassadors of Egypt, Pakistan, and Iran. Egyptian Ambassador Asraf Ghorbal was the first to volunteer. Egyptian nationals were among those being held at the Islamic Center. Ghorbal enlisted the aid of Pakistani Ambassador Sahabzada Yaqub-Khan and Iranian Ambassador Ardeshir Zahedi. Yaqub-Kahn and Zahedi were on the board of governors of the Islamic Center.

On Wednesday evening, the three ambassadors were brought to the MPD Command Center in the Municipal Building where they made a series of telephone calls to Khaalis. Yaqub-Kahn, a retired Pakistan army general with a Ph.D. from Harvard, did most of the talking for the ambassadors. He appealed to Khaalis' Islamic faith and read passages from the Quran that expressed peace, compassion, and mercy.

Reporters from all over the world also called B'nai B'rith. Wanting to get his message out to the public, the Hanafi leader told the media what had happened to his family and that those responsible had not been brought to justice.

Bob called home to say he wouldn't be able to leave the District Building until midnight—when his relief was expected. It looked like the takeovers would not end anytime soon. He emphasized that "patience" is the key strategy employed by police negotiators in such incidents. "Hostage takers are given time to cool off, so the situation can be defused," Bob advised. "Negotiators talk around demands that can't be met in order to keep the conversation moving in a positive direction and to buy more time to wear down the hostage takers."

To show good faith, authorities agreed to several of Khaalis' demands. They succeeded in halting the showing of the film *Mohammad, Messenger of God*. The film was pulled from New York theaters. Khaalis thought the film to be sacrilegious. And the $750 Khaalis paid in attorney fees for a contempt of court hearing during the 1973 murder trials was refunded to him by the city. To establish mutual trust, police agreed not to storm the buildings if Khaalis would not harm any more hostages.

The MPD official in charge at the District Building was Captain Robert Klotz, the Commander of the Special Operations Division. Klotz took Bob up to the fifth floor to view the scene. Dried blood could still be seen on the hallway floor. MPD officers armed with rifles and shotguns and wearing ballistic helmets and vests crouched behind conference tables that had been turned on their sides for makeshift barricades. The glass surrounding the double doors that led into the reception area of the council offices had been shot out. The doors themselves showed damage from gunfire as well as some of the inner walls. A female hostage could be seen sitting in a chair immediately inside the doorway of the office where the hostages were being held. Her arms were bound to the chair; she was being used to shield the movements of the two abductors.

On the return to the police command post, Bob reminded Klotz that British Prime Minister James Callaghan would be arriving at the White House South Grounds at 10:30 a.m. the following morning (March 10). It was the beginning of an official state visit. Bob was scheduled to work the arrival ceremony, which would include a 19-gun salute. The Presidential Salute Battery of the 3rd U.S. Infantry (The Old Guard) renders the honors for White House ceremonies. They utilize World War II vintage artillery, which fire a 75-millimeter blank shell containing a pound and a half of powder. The guns make quite a roar.

The hostages were being held in the northwest corner of the District Building, just off 14th Street and Pennsylvania Avenue.

There was nothing but open park area diagonally between that corner of the building and the White House South Grounds where the salute would be fired. Captain Klotz immediately picked up on Bob's concern and asked that the salute be canceled. The sound of the guns firing might spook the hostage takers into harming their captives.

Bob called the USSS Washington Field Office, the Presidential Protective Division White House Command Post (W-16), and the Department of State Office of the Chief of Protocol and relayed MPD's request. Bob received assurances from all that the salute would not occur.

The following morning, Bob reported to the South Grounds to serve as a PI team member for the arrival ceremony. He saw the Army cannon teams arrive at the Southwest Gate (B-3). The officer in charge said they decided to report to the White House "just in case." As the situation at the District Building had not been resolved, the salute battery returned to Fort Myer. It was the first time anyone could remember that the traditional salute honors had not been rendered.

After the arrival ceremony, Bob relieved the midnight agent at the police command post in the District Building. Later that afternoon, Ambassador Ghorbal invited Khaalis to meet with the ambassadors and police officials at a "table of peace." Khaalis consented to the meeting and preparations were made. A conference table was set up on the first floor of the B'nai B'rith building. Although Khaalis originally wanted to be armed and accompanied by several followers, he eventually agreed to come alone. It was also decided that none of the parties would bring weapons to the meeting.

At about 8:10 p.m. on Thursday evening, March 10, the trio of ambassadors along with Cullinane, Rabe, and Captain Joseph O'Brien, Commander of the MPD Homicide Division, sat down with Hamaas Abdul Khaalis. O'Brien participated in the meeting because he had maintained contact with Khaalis since the 1973 murders, and some trust had been established between the two.

During the talks, Chief Cullinane pronounced that it was beyond his control to present the murderers of Khaalis' family. At the same time, Ambassadors Ghorbal, Zahedi, and Yaqub-Kahn continued to appeal to Khaalis' orthodox Moslem beliefs. Citing Islamic principles of peace and goodwill, the Moslem diplomats reinforced on Khaalis the need to treat the hostages with compassion and mercy. The ambassadors also acknowledged Khaalis' great loss. They grieved with the Hanafi leader over the senseless murder of his family. To ease the tension of the standoff, the ambassadors reiterated that Khaalis had made his point. He had been successful in getting the story of the tragedy out to the world and in attaining most of his demands.

Khaalis finally came to the realization that the individuals he sought would not be brought to him—*no matter what.* For the release of the hostages, Khaalis next asked for immunity from prosecution for himself and his men. Cullinane replied that the Justice Department would *never* agree to that. Emphasizing that they were negotiating in good faith, police officials said they would *not* make promises they could not keep.

After three hours of discussion, police negotiators found an opening to end the crisis. A weary Khaalis expressed a desire to go home. Chief Cullinane and Deputy Chief Rabe seized the opportunity. They offered Khaalis a deal. If he and his men surrendered, Khaalis would be permitted to await trial at home. During arraignment, the government would ask that Khaalis be released on his personal recognizance (no cash).

In the early morning hours of Friday, March 11, Khaalis and his band of men laid down their weapons and surrendered at all three locations. The hostages were free after almost 40 hours of captivity. Some were taken to hospitals for medical treatment, while others were reunited with family and friends. Church bells tolled that morning as news of the hostage release spread throughout the city.

The hostage takers were transported to police headquarters and processed. Later that morning, they were arraigned in D.C. Superior Court. Most were held over for trial in lieu of hefty surety (cash) bonds. In accordance with the agreement to end the crisis, Hamaas Abdul Khaalis was freed without bond. He returned to his 16th Street residence. The terms of release stipulated that Khaalis must surrender his passport and not leave the District of Columbia. Khaalis also had to turn over any firearms that might be on the 16th Street property and to refrain from breaking any laws.

The release deal brought criticism from the public, some congressional leaders, and even a law enforcement official from a neighboring jurisdiction. They believed that deals made under duress should not be kept. Promise anything to end the crisis but don't bow later to extortion.

Bob, however, felt Cullinane and Rabe had done the right thing. The deal ended the crisis without further harm to any of the hostages. Bob said police found a small arsenal of weapons and over 10,000 rounds of ammunition when they searched the B'nai B'rith building. The Hanafis had to rent a box truck to transport it all. An execution room had also been readied at the B'nai B'rith site. Seven heavily armed men could have caused much murder and mayhem. Plus, there were two other hostage locations to contend with. Since one person had been killed at the District Building, police worried that Khaalis had been forced beyond the point of no return and would have nothing to lose if he carried out his threats.

Considering the circumstances, Bob thought the pretrial release for Khaalis was a small price to pay for a peaceful end to the standoff. Bob knew that the FBI had a court-ordered wiretap on Khaalis' phone and that MPD Emergency Response Teams had surveillance on Khaalis' residence. There was no danger that Khaalis would be able to flee prosecution or put into play some new terrorist plot.

Bob compared it to the way he dealt with protective intelligence subjects. It was important to establish trust and to keep one's word. "Most of these people are already pretty paranoid," Bob said. "If you lie to them, the next time they come in contact with me or another agent could spell serious trouble. The police are in the same boat in hostage situations. Once it gets out that police and government prosecutors don't keep their word, it'll make future hostage situations that more difficult to negotiate. Subjects will not believe anything the police say."

It took Hamaas Abdul Khaalis a little less than three weeks to violate the terms of his pretrial release. Khaalis threatened to kill people during several alarming telephone conversations that were overheard on the FBI wiretap. As threats to do bodily harm are a violation in the District of Columbia, Khaalis was arrested on March 31, 1977, and held without bond.

On July 23, 1977, a jury of ten women and two men found all 12 Hanafis guilty of multiple counts of armed kidnapping. Only Khaalis, as leader of the conspiracy, and the two individuals at the District Building were found guilty of second-degree murder. The three were also found guilty of assault with intent to kill. The *minimum* sentence handed out to the 12 Hanafis ranged from 24 to 78 years in federal prison. Hamaas Abdul Khaalis was sentenced to 41–123 years. He died in 2003 at the Federal Correctional Complex at Butner, North Carolina.

March 1977 presented the USSS with yet one more surprise. On March 24, First Lady Rosalynn Carter, accompanied by her personal secretary, slipped away from the White House for a secret shopping trip to New York City. Neither the Secret Service nor the first lady's press secretary was notified of the visit. Mrs. Carter shopped the fashion houses along Seventh Avenue.

Agents of the First Lady Detail only became aware of the situation when the New York Field Office (NYFO) called W-16 to check on the whereabouts of Mrs. Carter. The NYFO had received a report that the first lady had been spotted in the city.

The White House Communications Agency maintains a system of computer monitors that list the locations of the president, vice president, and other Secret Service protectees. The W-16 agent advised that the locator screen showed the first lady at the White House. At the same time, members of the White House press corps were calling the first lady's office to find out what was going on. The New York press was reporting that Mrs. Carter was in Manhattan.

With confusion mounting, the NYFO dispatched agents to check on the reports. They caught up with the first lady along Seventh Avenue. That evening, they escorted Mrs. Carter to LaGuardia Airport where agents accompanied her back to Washington.

Paired with Dick Corrigan, Bob worked the WFO-PI team that covered the first lady's arrival back at Washington National Airport. When he got home that night, Bob related how unbelievable the whole day had been. To think that the first lady could leave the White House unnoticed and that an aide would arrange a trip to New York without protection seemed almost impossible—especially only several weeks after the Hanafi takeovers. As unlikely as it may have been, that's exactly what happened. Bob was relieved that the first lady was back safely at the White House. The portion of the trip made without protection had exposed Mrs. Carter to potential danger by making her a target of opportunity.

Bob stayed very busy during 1977. His work never seemed to let up. He frequently served as the PI duty agent. We couldn't go anywhere when Bob was on call. He was often gone on a moment's notice, most of the time not returning for hours.

Saturday, April 23, was one of those days. Shep Kelly, a State Department SY agent and friend of ours, stopped by the house. Kelly was leaving SY and moving out of the area to take a position with the State of Illinois. Shep wanted to personally say goodbye.

We invited Shep to stay for lunch. I had just put some sandwiches on the dining room table when the telephone rang. "I hope it's not work," I cried out. Bob answered the phone and immediately reached for the pad of paper and pencil lying nearby. "Darn it, another Saturday ruined," I moaned.

A couple of minutes later, Bob returned the receiver to the cradle and turned to Shep and me. "I'm sorry," Bob said. "A bomb exploded this morning at Washington National. It was near the VIP gate. A man was killed. I have to go."

"Bob, do you mind if I follow you over? I'll get the info for SY. You know we use that area too," Shep said.

"Of course not, let me grab a suit and say goodbye to the kids."

"In the meantime, I'll call my Ops desk," Shep announced.

A short time later, Bob appeared with a hang-up bag over his shoulder. Not wanting to take the time to change, Bob was responding in casual clothes. But he always made sure he had a dress shirt, tie, and business suit with him—in case he would later have to work a protective assignment. "I'll call when I can," Bob promised. Then he kissed me goodbye.

Shep gave me a parting hug. "I want you guys to visit me in Springfield."

"Be safe," I called as Bob and Shep charged out the door with sandwiches in hand. Bob was off on another adventure.

Located on the Virginia side of the Potomac River, Washington National Airport first opened in June 1941. It stands on land once owned by George Washington's adopted stepson, John Parke Custis. The Main Terminal was designed with columns and other architectural accents influenced by Mount Vernon, Washington's beloved home.

Through the years, National grew into a major regional airport with over 10 million passengers using its facilities annually. The Main Terminal was expanded in 1950. In 1958, the new North Terminal opened followed by the Commuter Terminal in 1970. In 1998, the airport's name was officially changed to Ronald Reagan Washington National Airport.

Bob and Shep parked near the airport's VIP gate in spaces reserved for law enforcement vehicles. USSS motorcades used this entrance to pass directly to and from the tarmac. This allowed protectees to board and disembark aircraft without having to pass through waiting rooms and other public areas that were potentially dangerous.

Entering the nearby south extension of the Main Terminal, the two men made their way to a public corridor near the Eastern Air Shuttle waiting room. An FAA policeman directed them to a door that opened into a hallway within the restricted area of the building. There, they were met by the lead investigator, who was from the Alexandria Field Office of the FBI. The agent reviewed Bob and Shep's credentials and entered the identifying data in the Bureau's crime scene book. "You're just in time," the FBI man said. "You'll be able to see the room before it's hosed down. It's right around the corner. We're finishing our evidence collection and will be releasing the area to airport personnel."

Bob and Shep were then led into the scene of the explosion—a men's locker room used by the airport's custodial staff. There was a trail of dried blood on the floor, which led to an adjoining room. Powder burns could be seen on some of the lockers. There were marks on the ceiling and walls where shrapnel had been embedded. Some ceiling tiles were missing. They had been collected by the FBI as evidence.

"The bomb exploded at about 11:00 a.m. this morning," the lead FBI agent advised. "From the fragments, we believe the device was a pipe bomb—black powder packed into a three-inch-diameter pipe about eight inches long. The bomb was hidden in a gray-steel Craftsman toolbox, which had been placed in a shipping carton. The bomb was rigged to detonate when the toolbox was opened.

"The decedent was an airport janitor. He was either sitting in a chair with the toolbox in his lap or standing next to a table with the toolbox on top. When he lifted the lid to look inside, the bomb exploded. The decedent staggered through an adjoining kitchen to a supply room where he was found on the floor.

"From our preliminary investigation, we don't believe the decedent was the maker or the target of the bomb. He was 51 years old and had worked at the airport since 1970. He was a widower and lived by himself in Southeast, D.C. He was friendly and considered a good worker. He had no known enemies.

"Tracing his morning activities, we believe the decedent found the shipping carton somewhere within the Eastern Air Shuttle area or the FAA restricted area. Police have checked the remainder of the airport for explosive devises with negative results. No one has claimed responsibility for the bombing.

"The locker room is used by about 50 employees," continued the FBI agent. "Though the door to the FAA restricted area is not secured, there is a cipher lock on the locker room door. Our best guess is the device was intended for an individual or group of individuals. A pipe bomb set as an entrapment device [booby trap] is personal. A terrorist bomb directed against the airport would more likely have been constructed of dynamite or plastic explosives and detonated with a timing device.

"We're checking out FAA personnel and Eastern employees who work in the vicinity to see if one of them might have been the intended target. The only thing we've come up with so far is an incident that happened last night. An individual arrived late and missed the final shuttle flight of the evening to New York. Apparently, he became quite upset, and police were summoned. Eastern Air Shuttle doesn't require reservations. They guarantee that everyone who shows up for one of their hourly flights will get a seat—even if they have to add an additional plane and crew. But that doesn't apply to passengers who show up late."

The Bureau agent handed Bob a slip of paper with the subject's name and other identifying information. "The guy lives in D.C. Bill Thomas from our Washington Field Office is checking him out."

"I've worked with Bill on some cases," Bob said. "I'll give him a call."

When the briefing was concluded, Bob and Shep headed to the FAA Police office where they borrowed a couple of desks and phones. Shep informed SY of his findings, while Bob reported the information to the USSS Intelligence Division. Bob asked ID to run a record check on the subject who was involved in the Friday night incident. Bob almost fell out of his chair when he heard the results. An ID computer screen synopsis of the subject's criminal record revealed he had been convicted in 1970 of attempted first-degree murder and aggravated arson.

"Pull the subject's hard file," Bob said. "I'll be there in 15 minutes." Bob said goodbye to Shep and drove across the 14th Street Bridge to USSS Headquarters. After showing his credentials to the special officer on duty, Bob was buzzed into an inner hallway. Bob activated a four-digit cipher lock and entered the duty desk area of the USSS Intelligence Division.

Bob anxiously reviewed the subject's file. It contained police reports and newspaper clippings. Bob could hardly believe what he was reading. As a juvenile in 1970, the subject had apparently come under the influence of black revolutionary ideology. Police became suspicious of the individual after he was found injured near the scene of a bombing. Authorities suspected the subject had planted the device and that it detonated prematurely.

In the same Midwestern city 10 days before, a bomb had exploded in the women's restroom of a downtown department store. The device contained a two-pound stick of dynamite detonated by a timer. A woman was seriously injured in that blast, sustaining permanent injuries to her lungs. While police were checking the scene, they found another device hidden in a nearby locker, which fortunately had failed to detonate. This bomb contained 10 two-pound sticks of dynamite. Its purpose was to injure and kill the police and firemen who had responded to the first explosion.

On the day of the bombing, witnesses spotted a suspicious male—dressed as a woman—carrying a package into the department store. This individual's description was similar to the subject. Additionally, a friend of the subject informed police that the individual had bragged about planting the bombs. With this information, police applied for and received a search warrant for the subject's residence. Manuals on bomb making and urban warfare were found.

In the ensuing trial, the subject was convicted of attempted first-degree murder and aggravated arson. The subject was sentenced to 20 years. He served about three years in a state reformatory. After his release, subject moved to Washington, D.C. to pursue journalistic ambitions. The Secret Service had a file on the subject because he had been on the guest list for several White House functions.

Bob telephoned the Washington Field Office of the FBI and told the government operator that he was a Secret Service agent and needed to speak with Agent Bill Thomas as soon as possible. "Is this for real?" the duty operator asked incredulously. Bob gave the operator assurances that this wasn't a crank call.

A short time later, Thomas called Bob at the Intelligence Division. "Bob, Bill Thomas here. What's up, buddy?"

"Bill, I'm covering the National Airport bombing investigation for the Service. Headquarters is especially concerned since the gate we use for motorcades is at the south end of the Main Terminal. It's not known where the device was originally left or for whom it was intended. I just came from the scene and was told you're looking into a guy who was involved in an incident there last night."

"That's right. I'm at the field office getting my facts lined up before I take a run out to see him. The individual has felony priors in the Midwest. I'm getting an agent out there to see if he can pull local records on a Saturday. We might have to wait until Monday."

"Bill, I've got some good news for you. I have a copy of the subject's police file in front of me along with some newspaper accounts. He was convicted of a department store bombing. A device with a two-pound stick of dynamite activated by a timer went off in a women's restroom. A woman was seriously injured. An entrapment device was found hidden in a storage locker in the restroom—10 two-pound sticks of dynamite. Fortunately, it had a faulty timing mechanism and didn't explode."

"Holy crap!" Thomas cried out. "Bob, can I come over and take a look at the file?"

"Sure, come to the eighth floor of 1800 G and ask for me."

Thomas arrived at USSS Headquarters, and Bob escorted him to ID. "Ten two-pound sticks of dynamite," Thomas repeated several times. "That would have caused a lot of death and destruction." Thomas reviewed the subject's file and made detailed notes. "Ten two-pound sticks of dynamite," Thomas said once more while shaking his head. "This kid had a lot of anger."

"Yeah, he bought into the revolution in a big way," Bob expressed in agreement.

"Bob, let's go see if he's at home," Thomas said. Bill was a regular guy, and a rapport had developed between the two. Bill welcomed Bob's company. Besides providing backup, Bob offered an investigative perspective that was outside the Bureau. It also saved Thomas time. On the first case the two went out on, Bill told Bob: "This saves a lot of phone calls. You can see for yourself exactly what I'm doing on the case."

The agents arrived at the apartment building where the subject resided. It was typical of the thousands of multi-unit structures that sprung up in Washington on every vacant lot during the 1940s and 50s. Thomas rapped loudly on the subject's door four or five times and called out, "Hello, anyone home?" There was no answer from within. "Boy, I'd love to get inside and take a look around," Thomas remarked.

"Drop me back at headquarters first," Bob declared.

Thomas chuckled and said: "I was just wishing out loud. We don't do that anymore—really."

On the way back to 1800 G, Bob suggested: "Maybe this guy took a shuttle flight to New York this morning. That would have placed him at the airport. Even if he has no connection to the blast, he might have seen something."

"Yeah, I was thinking about that too. I'll get Alexandria to check with the airline."

Agent Thomas and Bob weren't able to find the subject at home until the following week. Cracking the door about a foot, the subject peered out at the two men. Bill held up his credentials and announced: "Agent Thomas from the FBI. We'd like to talk with you."

The subject immediately looked surprised and uneasy. "No, I don't speak with the FBI," he replied with some anger in his voice.

"Look, we need your help in a matter," Thomas explained.

"No, I'm not talking with you." The subject then shut the door on the two agents.

"That wasn't very friendly—was it?" Thomas remarked to Bob.

"No, he didn't act like someone whom the system has truly *reformed*," Bob replied.

"I think this guy still has a big chip on his shoulder," Thomas expressed.

The next day, Bill Thomas telephoned Bob with yet another twist. "Bob, I got a call from New York. You're going to love this. The subject's brother was arrested at LaGuardia Airport on December 28, 1975!"

A light bulb went off in Bob's head. "That was right around the LaGuardia bombing!" Bob cried out.

"You're good. It was the day *before* the blast," Thomas informed. "Some coincidence, huh."

With the subject's refusal to talk, many unanswered questions remained. Nevertheless, there was no hard evidence to link the subject to the National Airport bombing, and he was never elevated to suspect status. As with the LaGuardia explosion of 1975, the Washington National Airport bombing of 1977 remains unsolved to this day.

Also in 1977, Bob received a high-profile assignment as the PI coordinator for the Panama Canal Treaty signing between the U.S. and Panama. Bob spent many weeks preparing for the simultaneous state visits of 27 foreign dignitary protectees along with the security arrangements for the president and Mrs. Carter, former President Gerald Ford, and Lady Bird Johnson. Not since the state funeral of President Kennedy in 1963 had the Secret Service seen so many foreign leaders in Washington at one time.

Bob was tasked with the intelligence coordination for all 31 visits as well as the events pertaining to the treaty signing, which would take place at the Organization of American States (OAS) building. Bob was also assigned to cover all movements of Panamanian chief of government General Omar Torrijos during his visit to Washington.

In preparation, Bob spent days at the Intelligence Division reviewing the files pertinent to all protectees. He spent many hours checking with the FBI, State Department, CIA, and police in New York and Miami—and many hours more attending advance meetings and in other preparations. For the days leading up to the visits until their conclusion, Bob was like a ghost. I saw signs that he had been home, but I never caught sight of more than an apparition in the darkness of late night or early morning shadows.

Bob was concerned about the demonstrations planned to coincide with treaty events, but more worrisome was the potential for bombings. A thorough review of the past and present led Bob to believe that at least one bomb and possibly several would be detonated in Washington during the week of the treaty activities. This assessment was based on the history of certain anti-Castro Cuban exile organizations. Bob did not think they would pass up the opportunity that was being presented them. Thus, Bob's intelligence situation report warned of demonstrations, bomb threats, and bombings with the prediction it was "more likely than not that one or more bombs would be detonated in D.C. during treaty week."

Bob explained that on U.S. territory, the usual modus operandi of these groups was to explode a bomb late at night or in the early morning hours. Sites were targeted for the purpose of sending a powerful protest message and warning, while times of detonation were chosen to reduce the risk to innocent bystanders.

Bob noted that the embassies of OAS nations that have diplomatic relations with Cuba were of primary risk. Another potential target was the Cuban Interests Section, which had recently opened in D.C. In May 1977, the U.S. under the Carter administration had agreed to exchange "interests sections" with Cuba. While not a restoration of diplomatic relations, the interests sections would conduct consular matters. Diplomatic relations with Cuba were severed in 1961.

Of course, the OAS building, embassies of OAS members, and the Cuban Interests Section would be well protected during the treaty signing. And the Embassy of the Soviet Union, the nation that provided the most support to Cuba, was always well protected by the Secret Service's Executive Protective Service and under the surveillance of the FBI. Thus, Bob reasoned terrorists were more likely to select safer targets—as happened in May 1975 when a bomb exploded outside the Aeroflot (Russian airline) business office.

After Bob's situation report was received at USSS Headquarters, an intelligence research specialist (IRS) from the Foreign Intelligence Branch (FIB) called Bob. "What *hard* information do you have that bombs are going to be exploded in D.C. during treaty week?" she asked. "We didn't get anything about that from the FBI." Bob explained his rationale—as stated in the report—was based primarily on past activity. "So, your assessment is purely *speculative*," she said.

"I'd describe it as a credible prediction based on well-reasoned analysis," Bob replied.

General Torrijos arrived at Andrews Air Force Base on the evening of Monday, September 5. He and his family were transported by USSS motorcade to the Jackson Place residence of the Blair House complex where they would be the guests of President Carter. Later that evening, Bob gave a personal intelligence briefing to Torrijos' chief security aide, Lieutenant Colonel Manuel Noriega.

Twenty-six other heads of government/state and their delegations arrived in Washington on that Monday and Tuesday. Numerous motorcades crisscrossed the Embassy Row and downtown areas. Sirens wailed and emergency lights flashed in motorized movements choreographed by protocol and security. Washingtonians and tourists alike gazed at flag-bedecked limos—hoping to catch a glimpse of the international elite.

The official events of Panamanian treaty week began Tuesday evening at the Pan American Union building with a formal reception hosted by the OAS Secretary-General. About 1,500 guests attended. First Lady Rosalynn Carter represented the White House. President Carter spent the day in the Oval Office meeting bilaterally with a number of Latin American leaders.

During the early morning hours of Wednesday, September 7, Bob and I were awakened by a phone call from the WFO duty agent. Two bombs had exploded in D.C. One high-explosive device detonated at about 2:40 a.m. in a driveway behind the offices of the Soviet airline Aeroflot. No one was injured, but the shock wave of the blast blew out dozens of windows in nearby buildings, including the Capital Hilton Hotel and the Washington Post Building.

The other device exploded at about 3:00 a.m. on the northeast side of the Ellipse, near the Executive Office Building (EOB) and the White House. Although the blast was heard in the darkness, it took police some time to find the actual site of the bombing and to make sure no other bombs had been planted. It was eventually discovered that the bomb had exploded in a large concrete flowerpot that borders the Ellipse near E Street. The device caused property damage only; however, the blast would have been fatal to anyone standing within 20 feet of the explosion.

Anti-Castro Cuban exile groups took credit for the bombings. The first call came into the Washington Bureau of United Press International (UPI) at about 2:55 a.m. The caller claimed to be a member of the Pedro Luis Boitel Commandos (named after a student who died in a Havana prison in 1972). The caller stated they had just bombed Aeroflot and warned of bombs set near the White House. The subject condemned the Soviet Union for its support of Cuba.

The second call came into UPI's Miami Bureau at about 6:00 a.m. (when the office opened for the day). The caller claimed the Washington bombing was the work of the Cuban commando El Condor. The subject stated the bombing was in retaliation for giving away the Panama Canal to communists.

At daybreak, Bob responded to both crime scenes to observe the damage first hand and to gather the particulars. While he was at the site of the Ellipse blast, John Simpson, USSS Deputy Assistant Director (DAD) Office of Protective Operations (PO), arrived on the scene. Bob was on a first-name basis with the DAD. Simpson had previously served as the Special Agent in Charge (SAIC) of the Dignitary Protective Division (DPD). Bob had provided intelligence support for many of the foreign dignitary details headed by Simpson. DAD Simpson was a native of Boston, Massachusetts. With a syrupy New England accent, Simpson bestowed the title of "Brother" to those who had served under him.

"Brother Ritter," Simpson called out, "why here?"

"With the present level of security, this is about as close as you can get to both the OAS building and the White House without being detected," Bob answered. "To the perpetrators, this is a commando operation. An action here targets *both* the OAS and the U.S. The Cuban-exile groups aren't happy about our exchange of interests sections with Cuba and our plans to turn over the canal to Panama. They're also not happy with any of the nations that have relations with Castro Cuba, especially those within Latin America."

Bob noticed that Simpson looked worried. "John, cheer up. This is what we expected," Bob continued. "Fortunately, no one was injured by either blast. They've made their statement and gotten their headlines. We probably won't hear any more from them this week."

Simpson looked a bit surprised. "John, did you get a copy of my situation report on 'treaty week'?" Bob asked.

I read it," Simpson replied. "But I didn't believe it!"

Chapter 9

A Perplexing Mistake

Bob continued as a strong asset to the WFO-PI Squad. While all PI investigations can be dangerous, a few had some comic moments. In one instance, Agent Dick Corrigan was assigned a case that involved a check made payable to the president for a moderately large sum of money. A private citizen had mailed the check to the president on several occasions. Each time, the White House returned the check to the sender. When it showed up once again in the White House mailroom, the problem was turned over to the Secret Service.

First, Dick called the bank that the check was drawn on. Surprisingly, it was found that the subject had enough money in her account to cover the amount. Deciding to return the check in person, Dick asked Bob to accompany him. While Dick didn't think the individual was dangerous, it was always a good idea to have a witness along when contacting a female who might have mental problems.

During the drive uptown, Dick expressed: "I'm going to suggest she send the money to her favorite charity. Hopefully, this lady is just a bit eccentric and not a full-blown mental case."

"Yeah, if she has delusions of grandeur toward the president, we could have a problem on our hands. Right now, it seems her favorite cause is POTUS [President of the United States—pronounced pō-tus]," Bob reasoned.

Parking the government car near the apartment building where the subject resided, Dick and Bob took the stairs to the fourth floor. Police and federal agents never rode the elevators in residential buildings in certain neighborhoods. A couple of guys getting out of a plain four-door Ford sedan and dressed in suits and ties were a tip-off to wanted persons and juvenile trou-blemakers that "The Man" had arrived. If the power was turned off to the elevator during operation, law enforcement personnel could be trapped inside for hours, since the emergency phones inside the cab might also be inoperable.

Arriving at the subject's apartment, Dick rapped a couple of times on the door. From within, a woman's voice called out, "Who's there?"

"Mr. Corrigan, ma'am."

"What do you want?"

"I've been sent by the White House. I'd like to talk with you." Suddenly, the sound of footsteps could be heard inside the apartment. Reaching the door, the subject cracked it open to the length of the safety chain. She peered perplexingly at the two men. Holding his commission book to the opening, Dick an-nounced: "I'm Mr. Corrigan and this is Mr. Ritter. May we come in?"

Without saying a word, the subject unlatched the chain and motioned the visitors inside. She was in her mid-30s with a stocky build. "Ma'am, the White House sent us to personally thank you for your generosity," Dick declared. "It was a won-derful gesture." Pulling the check from his pocket, Dick contin-ued, "Unfortunately, the president isn't allowed to accept gifts such as this." Corrigan extended the check to the subject.

The subject's face changed from confusion to anger. "I want to give my money to the president. You take the check back," she commanded.

"Ma'am, your thoughtfulness toward the president is enough." Dick countered. "He'd like you to donate it to your favorite char-ity."

The subject snarled, "No, you tell the president to keep it."

Dick tilted his head back and forth toward the door, giving Bob a sign to start moving that way. Backpedaling to the door, Dick said in a soothing voice: "All right, ma'am, I don't want to argue with you. The White House can't accept this; we have to leave it with you. Please accept our regrets." With that, Corrigan dropped the check inside the apartment as he followed Bob out the door.

Bob and Dick headed down the hallway to the fire door. They hurried down the stairs. At about the third-floor landing, Dick and Bob heard the sound of quick footsteps hitting the steel treads above them. "Step on it, Bob; she's moving!" Corrigan shouted.

At the street, Bob and Dick ran for the government car, with the lady in hot pursuit, waving the check out in front of her. Just that moment, a Metropolitan Police cruiser came around the corner. Seeing the show before them, the MPD officers pulled to the curb. One of the officers called out with a chuckle, "Secret Service or FBI?"

Corrigan, somewhat embarrassed, pulled out his commission book and answered, "Secret Service."

At the same time, the subject threw the check at Bob, who was trying to get into the passenger side of the government vehicle. Then without fanfare or warning, she removed the skirt she was wearing and threw it on the sidewalk, revealing a full girdle. "What do I have to do," she screamed, "send my clothes to the president too!" Then she started to unbutton her blouse.

"No, no," Bob cried out. Knowing he and Dick were fighting a losing battle and only making things worse, Bob picked up the check and tried to calm the subject: "We'll take the check back. Please keep your clothes on."

Seeing the check in Bob's hand, the subject did an about-face and headed back to the apartment building, not bothering to pick up her skirt or to refasten her blouse.

"Do you need assistance?" the officer inquired, still smiling.

"No, I think we're okay now. I was afraid for a moment we might have to commit her," Corrigan answered.

Back at the office, Dick closed out the case by sending the check back to the White House with a suggestion that it be shredded.

Another humorous moment occurred when Bob and a female agent were sent on a Saturday afternoon to stake out the Sky

Terrace of the Hotel Washington (515 15th St., NW, D.C.—since renamed the "W"). The hotel's rooftop bar and grill overlook the Treasury Building and the White House. A waitress reported that while serving lunch to two male patrons, she overheard them trying to determine the distances from the bar to targets within the White House complex. It was recounted that the subjects had made the comments in the context of the range a sniper would zero in on. The waitress described the two subjects as in their mid to late 20s with medium length brown hair. The waitress also noted that one of the subjects said he would be back later that day.

Attired in casual clothes, Bob and the female agent took up a position at one of the tables and looked like any other young couple enjoying each other's company on a Saturday afternoon. They sipped tea from highball glasses, while they waited for the subject to return. As the afternoon progressed, the bar filled up with hotel guests, tourists, and others seeking refreshment and a birds-eye view of the city.

A person who brought some concern to the female agent suddenly entered the bar. "Oh, no! There's an agent I know from headquarters who just entered the bar," she informed. "We went through SS school together. I might have to go over and tell him we're working, so he doesn't blow our cover."

Just then, the HQ agent caught site of Bob's partner. Coming to the table, the agent loudly greeted her, "Hey, Sally, how's things over at the field office?"

The female agent responded softly, "Mark, this is Bob Ritter from WFO; we're here working an investigation."

"Sally, we're friends. You're here having a couple of drinks on a Saturday afternoon. I know the Secret Service hierarchy frowns on agents seeing each other. You don't have to worry about me; I won't tell anyone."

"Mark, we're not on a date. There's only iced tea in these glasses. Bob's happily married. We're working a PI investigation. A couple of guys were in here earlier talking about ranges to the White House for sniper shots."

"Now I believe you," the agent said as he sheepishly dipped his head. "That was Joel Murphy and I. We met for lunch." Bob and Sally looked over to see the waitress frantically confirming that the HQ agent was indeed the subject in question. All three agents had a good laugh over the double case of misunderstanding.

In June 1978, Bob suggested at a general office meeting that gun lockers be installed in the WFO prisoner processing area. Bob felt that agents should have the *option* of locking up their weapons before processing prisoners, so prisoners would not be able to snatch a weapon.

Several other agents had told Bob they would back him at the meeting. However, when Bob brought up the suggestion, the AT of the Criminal Squad scoffed at Bob and ridiculed the idea. The AT said words to the effect that anyone who couldn't control their own weapon shouldn't be an agent. With the AT's barrage of disparaging comments and others joining in on the attack, Bob's backers deserted him and remained silent. With no one supporting Bob, Special Agent in Charge Gerald Bechtle quickly dismissed the idea.

About a week later, two police officers from a local department (Prince George's County, Md.) were tragically shot and killed by a 15-year-old juvenile, who had been arrested for *petty* larceny. While the juvenile was being booked, he was able to strip the arresting officer of his weapon. The subject then fired three shots. One struck the arresting officer in the chest causing a fatal injury. Hearing the shots, two other officers rushed into the booking area. The juvenile opened fire on them with the remaining three rounds of the stolen revolver. One of the responding officers was mortally wounded.

Because of this double tragedy, SAIC Bechtle called a special office meeting. He said with some emotion: "We were all too quick to dismiss Bob's suggestion. I'm guilty like everyone else. I think we owe him an apology."

The SAIC then announced that several gun lockers would be ordered for the WFO processing area. Bob was moved by the SAIC's admission. There weren't too many Secret Service bosses who would stand up in front of a roomful of their subordinates and admit to an error in judgment.

In early summer of 1978, Bob was selected to be the PI agent for a protective survey team that would update procedures for visits to the President's Guest House (Blair House complex) and some of Washington's most popular convention hotels. He was happy to have received the assignment, as he would have significant input into the results.

After completing a long and detailed survey of the President's Guest House, the team turned next to the Washington Hilton Hotel. The hotel's management pressed for a change to the existing survey that would keep the hotel's T Street entrance open to the public at all times during a presidential visit.

Bob *strongly* advised against this and suggested ways to keep the area closed during presidential arrivals and departures, while minimizing the inconvenience to hotel guests. He was shocked when the lead survey agent, Dan Mitchell, bowed to the hotel's request.

The area would now be open to the public at all times. The Service would lose 360-degree coverage, as the president would now come as close as 15 feet or less to the rope line which marked the *unsecured* public area. Even worse, the president might be tempted to go to the rope line to shake hands with the public. That would permit a dead-on shot by an assassin with a handgun or serve as a "kill zone" for explosive detonations.

Bob's recommendation that presidential movements to hotels receive two PI team coverage was also rejected. The lead advance agent revealed, "I was told to reduce the number of agents, not add to it."

Bob went to the PI Squad supervisor, but he dismissed Bob's concerns outright. Next, Bob sought the advice of Bert de Freese, his first WFO supervisor. De Freese said he would have an *informal* talk with Mitchell, whom he had known for quite some time. Both men had been assigned to the Presidential Protective Division (PPD) earlier in their careers.

After the talk with de Freese, the lead agent added an extra PI team to the survey but kept the T Street entrance open at all times. The second PI team would give special attention to the area and cover the crowd during arrivals and departures. Bob was told Mitchell had run the changes by PPD-Operations and received their approval.

To Bob, it was unbelievable that experienced, able agents could not see the inherent danger in the change, especially since the president visits the hotel frequently. Bob's exact words to me were, "They're playing Russian Roulette with the president's life!"

To add to the problem, Bob was soundly reprimanded by the PI Squad AT. He wrongly concluded that Bob had taken his concerns *directly* to the Protection Squad AT, in defiance of a USSS unwritten rule that one does not go over the head of one's supervisor. Bob was immediately transferred to the WFO Forgery Squad.

When he arrived home that night, Bob was pretty much in despair. He told me he intended on pursuing the matter further.

Chapter 10

Forgery Squad

As upset as Bob was with the circumstances that had overtaken him, he was more worried about the changes to the Washington Hilton protective survey. Bob had completed several temporary duty assignments with the Presidential Protective Division. He was acquainted with a number of PPD agents. "I'm thinking about talking with one of the supervisors I know on PPD," Bob said.

"No, Bobbie, please don't do that," I begged. "You did all you could. They're not going to want to get involved. You'll only get yourself in more trouble."

"Yeah, you're probably right," Bob said reluctantly

"Bobbie, please promise me you won't do anything more about this. *Please!*"

"Okay, honey—I promise."

I didn't know then that this decision would later haunt Bob for the rest of his life. To be honest, I thought Bob was probably overreacting as to the potential danger the change might cause. Bob was an absolute perfectionist and believed in taking no chances. If Bob had his way, the president would *never* walk by an unscreened public area.

I knew Dan Mitchell. I had met him at office functions, and he had helped us during our house move. Dan was an outstanding person. Bob looked up to Dan as one of the top WFO agents and more importantly as a friend. It just didn't seem possible to me that Dan and his WFO superiors would do anything that would put the president in harm's way.

I had been approached before about Bob's tenacity. One of Bob's co-workers, Agent Barbara Riggs, had come to me at a

WFO Wives' Club meeting. Barb was concerned that Bob was taking the job too seriously. "Work is a means of supporting my avocation," Barb said. "It allows me to provide for my horses. I'd rather be out riding than here. Jan, you know I think the world of Bob, but I'm afraid he's going to burn himself out. He worries too much about work and especially things he can't change."

I knew Bob wouldn't burn out. He was on a calling and thrived on the challenges he faced. My candle, however, was burning down. Bob's time in the PI Squad had taken a toll on me. The past two and a half years had been an endless action-film serial of late-night call outs, long hours, no days off, and out-of-town travel.

The silver lining to the recent incident was Bob's transfer to the Forgery Squad. I hoped Bob would be able to keep hours that were more regular. There were about 40 agents in the WFO Forgery Squad, which was the largest and busiest in the Secret Service. In fact, the squad was larger than most USSS field offices.

Within the Washington area, millions of U.S. Treasury checks (T-checks) were issued each year to federal workers, military personnel, federal retirees, and Social Security recipients. Treasury also issued the payroll and public assistance (welfare) checks for the District of Columbia, since these were federal obligations.

This made for a huge pool of U.S. government checks available to be stolen from the mail, especially in the impoverished sections of Southeast and Northeast Washington. Add to this, the number of U.S. Savings Bonds stolen from the mail or in burglaries. A large squad was needed to investigate the endless stream of forgery cases referred to WFO from Treasury.

While the Postal Inspection Service investigates mail theft, the Secret Service has primary investigative jurisdiction for the forgery (signing to deceive) and uttering (fraudulent cashing) of U.S. government checks. Due to the fact most forged T-checks are stolen from the mail, postal inspectors and USSS agents often conduct investigations hand in hand. Local police also have a stake in these crimes, since state and D.C. theft and fraud statutes can come into play.

Because of its size, the WFO Forgery Squad was divided into five groups. No other squad was organized that way. Bob's group leader (GL), Jim Smith, seemed wary of Bob. Rumors circulated around the office that Bob had gotten in trouble with the PI Squad ATSAIC. In the retelling, misunderstandings became embellished. Who knows what was being whispered behind Bob's back?

Bob didn't receive much of a welcome from Smith. Bob was curtly told to pick out an empty desk in the forgery bullpen and to be ready to start receiving cases. Since Bob was one of the few agents to reside in Maryland, he was assigned to cover a large section of Prince George's County (P.G. Co.) and the bordering sections of D.C. That was fine with Bob. He wanted a territory he could call his own.

Immediately, Bob paid a visit to the Prince George's County Police Check and Fraud Squad to establish liaison. He received an unexpected and very cold reception. The sergeant of the squad flatly stated that no one wanted to work with the Secret Service anymore. "Why?" Bob asked.

"The agent you're replacing couldn't be trusted," related the sergeant. "He had agreed not to make any arrests in a joint case until the investigation was played out. Your agent comes back from an out-of-town assignment and needs some stats. He pops a couple of arrests in the case. This tipped off several other suspects that we had an interest in for local offenses. They've fled the area; our case was ruined. We wasted a lot of time and effort."

"I apologize for that," Bob said. "I don't operate that way. I'm a former police officer and respect the sovereignty of local law enforcement. I understand your concerns and wouldn't do anything that we didn't have a consensus on."

The sergeant and Bob talked for another five minutes—with Bob trying to allay the sergeant's fears. Softening a bit, the sergeant introduced Bob to Detective Rich "Rabbit" Donnelly, the investigator who handled check fraud. Bob eventually won over the sergeant and Donnelly. Bob promised to cooperate fully and pledged to make no arrests in shared cases without Donnelly's concurrence.

With the fire out, Bob returned to the field office and stopped by to talk with Group Leader Smith. "I wish you would have warned me about P.G. County Check and Fraud, so I would have been prepared," Bob said. "When I went out there, I was told they didn't work with the Secret Service anymore."

Smith acted like Bob was delusional. "They couldn't have said that," Smith maintained. "I straightened that problem out myself."

"I don't make this stuff up," Bob said. "They were ready to show me the door. Call Sergeant Bender if you don't believe me."

Smith backpedaled, "Maybe they were just playing with you."

"No," Bob stated. "They were angry."

Smith continued to dismiss Bob's concerns and contended that nothing wrong had been done anyway. "We needed to make the arrests," Smith declared. "We can't sit on federal felonies forever."

Bob then realized that Smith had probably pressed for the arrests and was trying to play down the ill will it had generated. "Anyway, I smoothed things over," Bob said. "I'll keep us on good terms."

On the way back to the bullpen, Bob silently vowed to treat his local law enforcement partners as equals. Bob would keep the cases he worked jointly "close to the vest." He would tell the group leader as little as possible regarding those investigations. Keeping the GL in the dark would prevent him from pressuring for premature arrests.

Bob's next visit was to Largo, Maryland where Postal Inspector William "Bill" Solomon had his office. Bill's investigative territory included Prince George's County and Southern Maryland. Bill was happy to see some new Secret Service blood. The two hit it off right away. Bill offered to notify Bob whenever there were any mail thefts. Bob volunteered to give Bill an investigative hand. Solomon mentioned that he often worked with Detective Donnelly. Bob suggested that the trio meet for lunch.

The following Friday afternoon, Bob, Bill, and Rich gathered at the Shady Oak Inn in District Heights, Maryland. Each of the three talked about their professional lives. Bill Solomon was a couple of years from retirement. He longed for one more big case. Rich Donnelly was a corporal, who hoped to make sergeant. All shared a burning desire to clear the streets of criminals.

The theft and criminal negotiation of someone's payroll, public assistance, or Social Security check wreaked financial havoc on that individual and their family. It could be a month or more until a replacement check could be sent. A claim form had to be filled out, sent in, and reviewed before a new check could be cut. The Secret Service was often required to submit a "settlement report" before Treasury issued a substitute check. This report verified that the rightful payee had neither received the check nor cashed it. For folks living from check to check, any delay in payment was a severe personal hardship.

Bob suggested that the three men work together as a team. Bob reasoned that the criminals they were after touched all of their investigative jurisdictions. Bob pledged to work tirelessly with Bill and Rich to run out any and all leads. Bill and Rich liked what they heard. In the past, too many Secret Service agents had been part-time investigators, letting their casework slide when hit with protective assignments. Bob promised to do "whatever it takes."

The major problem with forgery investigations is that they're "cold cases" from the start. By the time the Secret Service receives the case, it's been weeks and in some instances months since the crime. The trail is stone cold. Most of the people who handled the transactions don't remember them. If they didn't note a physical description or some identifiers on the check, there was usually no information regarding the presenter.

Over the next six months, Bob worked with Rich Donnelly and Bill Solomon in Maryland. Within D.C., Bob partnered with Postal Inspector John Sternberg. Bob and John were college fraternity brothers and old friends. During one investigation in the field, Sternberg nostalgically remarked, "Bob, when you and I were throwing down beers together at The Varsity Grill, did you ever think we'd be running down bad guys together in Southeast D.C.?"

Bob closed his share of cases and made some arrests, but the vast majority of cases he was assigned contained no significant investigative leads. These cases had to be closed unsolved. Bob saw a pattern developing. Good identification appeared to have been used when uttering the forged checks. Most of the checks were cashed at "mom and pop" liquor stores and convenience marts that did not have transaction cameras. The description of subjects presenting the checks, when available, varied greatly. A large number of checks had been forged and uttered in this manner. Bob believed this pointed to an organized check-cashing ring. Bill Solomon and Rich Donnelly thought Bob might be onto something.

During the summer of 1978, a string of U.S. Postal Service (USPS) vehicles were broken into at various locations in North-east and Southeast, D.C. and P.G. Co. Md. The modus operandi was the same; the side windows of USPS Jeeps were forced open and mail bags stolen. The dates of break-ins coincided with the delivery dates for U.S. government checks. Bill Solomon and Bob decided to employ an old and basic investigative tool: the neighborhood canvass.

Bob and Bill canvassed the areas in Maryland where the vehicle break-ins had occurred. The two agents hoped to gather some leads while the trail was still hot. Pounding shoe leather and knocking on doors is a laborious, time-consuming technique, especially on sultry summer days. A week's worth of work and a pound of sweat went by with no information developed.

Then, Bob took a run out to a Prince George's County neighborhood where a number of T-checks had turned up missing in the past. The section had rural-type mailboxes affixed to posts. Bob circulated the area, asking if anyone had seen anything suspicious. Some hours later, Bob caught the break he needed. One resident had seen a young man in his 20s driving through the area following a mail truck on its delivery route. The subject was opening the mailboxes and inserting flyers. The eyewitness thought the action to be suspicious because the subject seemed to pause at each of the boxes longer than necessary. "Like he was going through the mail?" Bob asked.

"Exactly," answered the witness.

Bob got a description of the subject and his vehicle. Luckily, the witness still had one of the flyers. It was an advertisement for a Prince George's County nightclub. Investigation at the club yielded the subject's identity. The subject was name checked with no record found. An operator's permit check revealed the subject's residence. Bob contacted Bill Solomon and Rich Donnelly with the information. It was decided that the three would attempt to interview the subject that evening.

The individual resided in a garden-type apartment complex in Hillcrest Heights, Maryland. The subject would not invite the officers in; he preferred to talk at the door. After being advised of his Miranda rights, subject stated he delivered flyers for local businesses. He denied any involvement in mail theft. When told he was spotted following a postal truck and lingering at mailboxes, the subject claimed that he always tried to time his service with the mail delivery. This allowed him to insert the flyers within the postal bundle, so the advertisements would be taken into the recipient's home with the day's mail.

Bill Solomon started to close out the interview, "Okay, we'll be back in touch if we need anything else."

Bob wasn't buying it. "No one works that hard for a couple of cents a flyer," Bob asserted. "You're going through people's mail looking for T-checks. Look, I'll give you one chance to come clean with me, and I'll do what I can to help you. If we go the full 10 rounds, I'm going to work even harder to put you away for as long as possible."

"Whoa, Bob!" Solomon interjected. "It's been a long day." Solomon then gave one of his business cards to the subject and concluded the interview.

The three investigators gathered in the parking lot by their cars. "You think he's dirty, Bob?" Solomon asked.

"Yes, he's not taking all that time just to insert flyers."

Solomon turned to detective Donnelly, "What do you think, Rabbit?"

"I think it was a line of crap too," Donnelly replied.

"Okay," Solomon uttered, "I guess I'm getting old—and soft. I almost believed the kid."

"Here's what we'll do," Solomon advised. "Rabbit, I'll meet you at your office at 8:00 in the morning. We'll run out here and pick this kid up. We'll take him to the Postal Inspection office in D.C.

"Bob, you drop by at 11:00. That'll give Rabbit and me some time to work on him first. We'll be the good cops. If we can't break him, he won't have any problem seeing you as the bad cop," Solomon expressed with a chuckle.

The following morning, Solomon and Donnelly began the interrogation of the subject. "Agent Ritter's pissed at you," Solomon warned. "I wouldn't want that man on my ass. He's with the Secret Service. He doesn't have the time for your crap. Not only does he investigate federal crimes; he also has to protect the president.

"Agent Ritter's coming over here later. The only chance you have of staying out of jail is to cooperate with Detective Donnelly and me. Tell us everything you know, and if you're truthful we'll see what we can do. Otherwise, we're going to hand you over to Agent Ritter.

"He plans to arrest you for violation of 18 U.S.C. 1725, placing *unstamped* matter in a mailbox," Solomon continued. "He's got an ironclad case. Every mailbox you put a flyer in is an additional count.

"He'll put you in cuffs and take you to his office where you'll have to give handwriting samples until your fingers fall off. After you've been interrogated, printed, and photographed, it'll be too late for you to see a judge today. You'll spend the night in Central Cell Block. The drunks and weirdos will love to get a piece of you."

Solomon and Donnelly had never seen a suspect fold so quickly. "Okay, I'll tell you what you want to know. Just don't let Agent Ritter take me!" The subject then proceeded to give details about a large check-cashing ring that had been operating in the region for the past year and a half. Solomon and Donnelly couldn't take down the information fast enough.

For a chance to plea to lesser crimes and a probation recommendation, the subject was willing to become an informant and to provide incriminating evidence on a continuing basis. The subject claimed that some members of the ring were also into burglaries, robberies, drug dealing, stolen cars, credit card fraud, fencing, counterfeiting, financial schemes, white-collar crime, and prostitution.

Donnelly suggested to Postal Inspector Solomon that MPD Detective Robert Pleger be brought into the case. Donnelly vouched for Pleger's ability and integrity. Having Pleger onboard would gain a valuable ally within the Metropolitan Police Department, whose cooperation would be needed.

Bill Solomon called Bob to tell him the good news. "Our man's spilling his guts over here. You got us a good break, Bob. You were right about the check ring. This is going to be a huge case!"

The next day, Inspector Solomon drove a Postal Inspection Service surveillance truck around Prince George's County Maryland and Southeast D.C. In the back, Bob along with detectives Donnelly and Pleger debriefed the informant. The subject directed the law enforcement officers to locations where mail had been stolen and to businesses where checks had been uttered. The informant also led our men to recreational playgrounds and other hangouts where subjects involved in the ring frequented. The informant revealed that the public basketball courts of D.C. had become open-air markets for drugs and meeting places for criminals.

From the truck's one-way windows, Bob took pictures of suspects, while Rich and Robert noted identifying information. The informant described a criminal ring of about a dozen primary members. Over 50 others were used as needed in the criminal negotiation of the checks. Most of the participants were drug addicts.

One piece of information stuck in Bob's mind. The informant mentioned that a ring member known only as "Clay" had worked at an area bank. The informant did not know the name or location of the bank.

Bob had a hunch. That evening, he worked late at the office going through the check forgery photostats for the past year. He struck pay dirt. Bob discovered that over 50 District of Columbia pay roll checks had been fraudulently negotiated at a particular Northern Virginia branch of a major bank. Closer examination revealed that six of the checks had been cashed at the branch on the same day! Also noted was the fact that the branch was not near any of the mailing addresses on the checks. In fact, the addresses on the checks varied greatly in geographical location and did not coincide with the mail routes where USPS vehicles were broken into. These facts suggested two things to Bob: (1) There was a "dirty" teller at the bank branch; (2) The checks were stolen *before* they were mailed—probably out of a D.C. Government payroll office or mailroom.

The following morning, Bob met with the bank's head of security at their headquarters location in downtown D.C. The security chief, a retired FBI agent, checked the bank's transaction records regarding the checks in question. As Bob had suspected, one teller had handled all of the transactions. The teller was identified as Clayton Davis. The subject had worked for the bank for six months and then suddenly quit. "He probably didn't want to press his luck," Bob theorized.

"Yes, and you've given me pause for thought," voiced the security chief. "We're going to have to figure out a way to catch this type of thing in the future."

"So are we," Bob said.

During the next several months, Bob carefully reviewed the statements given by the informant. There were many pages of leads to run out. Bob checked the WFO photostat file for checks that were cashed at locations favored by the ring. He hoped to associate the cases through handwriting analysis to known forgers. Bob worked with the Forgery Squad agent who was a questioned document expert. WFO indices were searched for the individuals named by the informant as ring members.

Second endorser interviews were conducted at the businesses that had cashed the forged checks. When a suspect was developed, Bob showed a "photo spread" to the person who had handled the transaction. Bob would *spread* out pictures of 10 different individuals. One of the photos was of the suspect. The witness would be asked if he or she recognized any of the photos.

Persistence and hard work paid off. Several male and female forgers were positively identified and additional suspects were developed. A good number of forged and uttered checks were consolidated into Bob's parent case. Bob requested the original checks from the Check Claims Division (CCD) of the Department of Treasury. The checks would be sent to the U.S. Postal Crime Laboratory for handwriting and latent finger and palm print analysis.

The U.S. Attorney for the District of Columbia designated the ring an "organized crime group" operating within the Washington Metropolitan Area. Two AUSAs were assigned to coordinate the investigation and prosecution of ring members. The AUSAs directed the continuing undercover operations of the informant. The investigative team was compiling a wide array of evidence for presentation to the grand jury of substantive violations by a number of group members.

Bob was in the middle of all of this when he came home one evening in December 1978. While Bob and I shared a late dinner, I asked him his thoughts on the Jonestown, Guyana tragedy, which had been in the headlines for several weeks. On November 18, 1978, Congressman Leo J. Ryan (D-California) was assassinated in Port Kaituma, Guyana. Four persons traveling with Ryan were also murdered (including three members of the media); ten others were wounded.

At the time of the assault, Ryan and his party were attempting to depart Port Kaituma via two chartered aircraft. Representative Ryan had made a fact-finding trip to Jonestown, Guyana, an agricultural cooperative established by the charismatic Reverend Jim Jones and his Peoples Temple (no apostrophe). Complaints from relatives of some of Jones' followers prompted the inquiry. It was charged that members were being kept at Jonestown against their will and that living conditions had become intolerable. Ryan's party was comprised of staff, news media, concerned relatives, and an official from the U.S. Embassy.

The Ryan delegation arrived at Jonestown on November 17. They were given a tour of the facility and talked with Peoples Temple members. By the afternoon of November 18, about 15 persons let it be known that they wished to leave Jonestown. Congressman Ryan was going to stay one more night, while the remainder of the party would fly back to Guyana's capital city, Georgetown.

Through the State Department, Ryan arranged for the defectors to depart Jonestown with the official party. One Jonestown family was split about leaving. While the husband and wife argued, a Peoples Temple member suddenly assaulted the congressman with a knife. The attacker was subdued without any injury to Ryan.

With tensions running high, the State Department official traveling with Ryan ordered the congressman to proceed immediately with the official party and defectors to the airstrip at Port Kaituma. After one of the aircraft was boarded, a "supposed" defector opened fire on the passengers with a handgun. Two persons were wounded before the gun jammed. At the same time, a contingent of Peoples Temple security men suddenly appeared at the other aircraft and began the murderous assault on Congressman Ryan and his group. After the attackers left the scene, survivors hid in the jungle until their later rescue by the Guyanese army.

Back at Jonestown, Jim Jones was putting into action his "White Night" plan for the mass suicide/murder of the Peoples Temple flock. Under the constant urging of Jones, the inhabitants of Jonestown filed by a large vat where they were given cups containing a grape-flavored drink laced with cyanide. The poison was first administered to the children. Some of the adults voluntarily committed suicide. Others were coerced to drink by armed security guards. Some were injected with the poison. Several were shot. When the White Night ritual was completed, over 900 men, women, and children lay dead.

"It makes no sense to me why mothers would kill their children and why so many would end their lives," I told Bob.

"It was a socialistic cult founded on the principles of Marxism with apocalyptic overtones," Bob stated. "Jim Jones used control techniques—financial, psychological, physical, situational, and the like—to exert absolute power over his followers. They were reborn with Jones and believed he was a prophet. Jones substituted himself for religion. He was seen as the one and only true and legitimate leader, and his orders went unchallenged.

"The Secret Service is actually involved with the remnants of Jones' Peoples Temple. There's been an allegation some members are planning to assassinate certain American politicians. Supposedly, they're upset at what they believe was U.S. government persecution of the sect and want retribution."

"Really," I said.

"Yeah, the FBI and Service are looking into it," Bob advised. "The Bureau has also sent us a copy of an audio tape that was recorded during a portion of the suicides. I saw some of the transcript. Jones was extremely paranoid. He became resolute when told of Congressman Ryan's assassination. Jones warns his followers they'll be assaulted and tortured for the killing of the congressman. He orders the mass suicide as a way to defeat their enemies and as a vehicle for transformation to a better world. Jones uses the term 'revolutionary suicide.' Their deaths would be a final act of protest and also an escape.

"Jones had his temple practice the White Nights on previous occasions," Bob continued. "For some time, Jones had prophesized that the Peoples Temple was going to be attacked by outsiders. Apparently, he had thought about moving his temple to Cuba or the Soviet Union. Jones was seeking a socialistic Utopia. But in his paranoia, he moved closer to his self-fulfilling prophecy of apocalyptic confrontation.

"With Congressman Ryan's visit, Jones became more desperate. He was afraid of governmental intervention from both the U.S. and Guyana. It disturbed him greatly that some of his followers deserted him. The assassination of the congressman sealed the fate of the Peoples Temple."

"What could have been done to prevent this?" I asked.

"It's my understanding that authorities had been advised of the White Night suicide exercises but did not take them seriously. I certainly would have. People don't practice something that they don't intend on putting to use someday. To me, it wasn't a matter of if but a matter of when.

"Taking concerned relatives and press into Jonestown certainly aggravated Jones' paranoia and was probably seen by him as an invasion. But the fatal mistake I believe was Congressman Ryan's decision to arrange for the Jonestown defectors to depart with his official party. Jones' strictest rule was that one does not leave the Peoples Temple. The defectors were seen as traitors. Jones was worried they would reveal the true story to the world, and Jonestown would be destroyed. I believe Jones was already somewhat suicidal, and the congressman's assassination left him no way out. Honey, Jim Jones was *desperate*, and you know what I always say."

"Yes, desperate people are dangerous people!" I recited.

The New Year saw more upheaval in Iran. Mass demonstrations and nationwide strikes had plagued the country since August 1978. The Iranian students were getting their wish. On
January 16, 1979, the shah and his wife left Iran for Egypt.
Prime Minister Shahpour Bakhtiar was appointed by the shah
to establish a civilian government to institute reforms in Iran.
At the same time, the exiled Ayatollah Ruholla Khomeini was
plotting a return to Iran and the establishment of an Islamic re-
public.

In January 1979, Bob was called into SAIC Bechtle's office.
"Sit down, Bob," Bechtle said as he motioned to a nearby chair.
"I've got a special assignment for you. I know you have a major
forgery case, but I need you on an important intelligence matter."

Bechtle tossed a teletype to Bob. "As you know from your PI
time, a militant wing of the Iranian students operates out of
Northern Virginia. The FBI has information that they're planning a takeover of the Iranian Embassy in D.C. The Bureau's
Alexandria office has the investigation.

"You've established good liaison with the FBI in the past. I
need you to monitor the FBI investigation as closely as possible.
Headquarters is going *ape* over this. Your job will be to see that
the Bureau gives this a 'good shake' and that we get everything
they develop. Don't let them 'spin you,'" cautioned Bechtle.
"Both of our careers could depend on the job you do.

"You already know that the Bureau plays foreign and domestic
intelligence cases close to the vest," Bechtle continued. "Recently, our agents have complained about the lack of information they've been receiving. The FBI has been disclosing very
little as to the actual investigation conducted, often citing the
Attorney General's guidelines, privacy restrictions, or national
security regulations. A lot of cases are being closed with the FBI
field agent simply saying that FBI Headquarters has decided no
further investigation is warranted."

"Sir, I believe that's a reaction to the ongoing federal prosecution of former Director Gray and the two other FBI officials [Mark Felt and Edward Miller] for civil rights violations. The current FBI hierarchy doesn't have a clear and consistent view as to what is and isn't permissible in intelligence investigations. They're afraid of doing something now and being prosecuted for it in the future. So, they're doing, documenting, and disclosing as little as possible. I think it's also a bit of a silent protest. They're opening up fewer intelligence cases and not investigating them as fully as in the past."

"That's a fair assessment of the situation," Bechtle stated. "For this case, I want you to establish liaison *directly* with the SAC of the Alexandria office, Bob Kunkel. You'll be personally representing me and Director Knight."

"I'm to say I'm *personally* representing Director Knight?" Bob asked with some disbelief.

"Yes, so you're not blocked as to national security information and as a means of showing how important this is to us. For this case, you have 'need to know' and access as the director would. When they ask you if you have this and that access and have been read into this or that program, you say yes. They've been playing games like that with our agents. Headquarters has approved this, and Liaison has been advised."

"Okay, I understand," Bob replied.

"Are you familiar with Kunkel's background?" Bechtle asked.

"Yes, sir, he used to be the SAC of the Bureau's Washington Field Office. He got in trouble in the early 70s with then Director Gray. There was an incident on the Capitol grounds where an undercover FBI agent was overpowered by some anti-war demonstrators and had to be rescued by other agents. It was alleged that guns were drawn. Kunkel was accused of glossing over the incident. Apparently, he was censured and reassigned to Alexandria, a much smaller and less important office."

"Yes, and he was the Washington SAC during the initial Watergate investigation," Bechtle pointed out. "Some suggest that he didn't play ball with the White House and that was the *real* reason for the transfer."

"I'll keep that in mind," Bob said.

"I want *daily* updates," Bechtle ordered. "Any questions?"

"No, sir, I'll get right on this."

Bob headed back to his desk where he called the Alexandria Field Office of the FBI and requested an appointment with SAC Kunkel. The following morning, Bob arrived at Kunkel's office. He was greeted by the FBI agent who was the "security officer" for the Alexandria office. After checking Bob's credentials, the FBI security man announced: "We've already verified your TS clearance with SCI eligibility. The boss would like me to check on your special access authorizations."

"No problem," Bob replied.

After he satisfactorily answered all of the FBI agent's questions, Bob was ushered into SAC Kunkel's inner office. Kunkel rose from behind a massive mahogany desk and extended a hand to Bob. After exchanging handshakes, Kunkel invited Bob to sit down. "What can I do for you?" Kunkel asked as he peered at Bob from behind a pair of large-framed black glasses, which accented the FBI-SAC's silver-gray hair.

"Sir, I'm here on behalf of Secret Service Director Stu Knight and WFO-SAIC Jerry Bechtle. They send their warm regards and request your assistance in a matter that is currently being investigated by your office. It pertains to intelligence sent to Director Knight from the FBI regarding a militant group of Iranian students who are operating in your district. The information alleges that some members are planning a takeover of the Iranian Embassy.

"As you know, the Secret Service is responsible for the protection of the Iranian Embassy. The situation at the embassy is already tense. The new civilian government in Tehran stands in opposition to those who strive for a theocratic Iran and a clean break from the shah. The diplomats and military attaches at the

Iranian Embassy are jockeying for survival. Throw Iranian students into the mix and the violence and bloodshed in Iran could be transformed to D.C.

"Director Knight and SAIC Bechtle have asked me to personally relay their concern regarding the intelligence your office has developed. They sincerely appreciate your cooperation in the full investigation and resolution of this matter. The director has tasked me to be his 'eyes and ears.' The director requests that I have full access to the investigation, so I may keep him and SAIC Bechtle personally advised on a continuing basis."

"I understand your concerns," Kunkel affirmed, "but we weren't planning on doing much more on this. We reported the informant's allegations and planned to keep a lookout for anything more concrete. This is the kind of information that we probably wouldn't open a full intelligence investigation on until a law was violated."

"Sir, has your source proven to be reliable in the past?" asked Bob.

"Yes," answered Kunkel.

"The name of the game for us is prevention and preparedness," Bob remarked. "If a reliable informant is reporting that criminal activity is being planned for the Iranian Embassy, the director would respectfully request that everything that is legal and ethical be done as soon as possible.

"Earlier this month, Iranian militants stormed the home of the shah's mother and sister in Beverly Hills, California," Bob stated. "Fires were started; a police car was overturned; rocks and bottles were thrown, and over 30 persons were hospitalized."

Kunkel thought for a moment. "I met Director Knight a couple of times when he headed up your Washington office. At the time, I was the SAC of our WFO. If he's that concerned about this, we'll go ahead and open up an investigation for you."

"Thank you, sir. The Secret Service is in your debt," Bob said with sincerity.

Kunkel summoned a supervisory agent from the squad that handled domestic intelligence. Kunkel authorized the agent to initiate a full intelligence investigation into the informant's allegations. The agent was directed by Kunkel to allow Bob complete access to the investigation.

The supervisor took Bob to the squad area and introduced him to the case agent who would be handling the investigation. The three men discussed the case and how the investigation would proceed.

For the next 10 days, Bob worked his forgery cases and maintained close liaison with SAC Kunkel and the lead FBI agent. Bob stopped by the Alexandria office several times a day. He was given unprecedented access to the ongoing investigation. This included actually being taken to an FBI surveillance post, while it was operational. Bob was also permitted to talk with the FBI's confidential informant over the phone, so Bob could make his own assessment of the subject. Bob made sure he thanked Kunkel frequently for the excellent cooperation.

Bob briefed SAIC Bechtle daily. Toward the end of the investigation, Bechtle seemed worried. Bob tried to assure the SAIC that everything that could legally be done was being done. Bechtle said he'd like to accompany Bob on one of his visits to SAC Kunkel—just to be safe. "Believe me, boss, you know everything the FBI knows, but it would be a nice gesture for you to personally thank Kunkel for his help." Beaming a wide smile toward Bechtle, Bob stated, "At the same time, you can confirm for yourself the *terrific* job the FBI and I have been doing."

The following morning, Bob drove to the Alexandria Field Office. He asked Kunkel's secretary if it would be all right to bring SAIC Bechtle by that afternoon. She looked at Bob and broke out laughing. "What's so funny?" Bob asked.

"That's a really *odd* request for us," she replied. "In the FBI, there's a *strict* pecking order among SACs that correlates to field office size. The SAC of our WFO would *never* drop by here.

He'd be insulted if it was even suggested. Mr. Kunkel would be summoned over there."

"I see," Bob said.

The secretary looked at Kunkel's appointment book. "His schedule is clear this afternoon."

"I'll get Mr. Bechtle here around 1:00 p.m.," Bob advised.

Kunkel's secretary flashed Bob a skeptical look. "I'll believe it when I see him walk through the door," she said.

Later that day, Bob and SAIC Bechtle arrived at the Alexandria Field Office of the FBI and proceeded to SAC Kunkel's office. After Bob introduced Bechtle to Kunkel's secretary, she laughed and shook her head a couple of times. "It's an FBI thing," Bob told Bechtle. "I'll explain it to you later."

Meanwhile, Kunkel had seen the two Secret Service men outside his office and invited them in. Bob introduced his SAIC to Kunkel, who asked both men to take a seat. Bechtle handed Kunkel a business card and then swung a foot into the side of a nearby couch. "I just came over to kick my batteries," Bechtle said with a grin. The FBI-SAC smiled at Bechtle, who was joking that Kunkel's office had been "bugged" by the Secret Service.

"I want to thank you for the cooperation you've given us in this investigation," Bechtle began. "I really appreciate it. As Bob has told you, this is a very important matter to the Service. Bob's been keeping us informed, but I wanted to personally touch base with you to be sure we haven't missed anything," Bechtle told Kunkel.

"Your boy's been living over here," Kunkel declared. "I've been in the Bureau since 1942, and I can't remember anyone outside the FBI being granted more *operational* access to one of our sensitive intelligence investigations. We've done everything that's permissible, and he's been a shadow to my agents. It wouldn't surprise me if Bob showed up on payday looking for a check."

Bechtle laughed. The two top agents then discussed the Iranian situation. Bechtle and Kunkel concluded with some friendly "small talk" and promised to continue to collaborate in matters of joint interest.

Bob continued with the investigation of his major forgery case. By summertime, numerous arrests had been made with a sizable number of defendants convicted. An organized crime ring responsible for the theft of over a quarter of a million dollars had been brought to justice. Ringleaders were either behind bars or on the run. It had been the biggest mail theft and forgery ring that anyone could remember.

With that success under his belt, Bob was told he was being transferred to the Service's Intelligence Division.

Chapter 11
Intelligence Division

I n August 1979, Bob reported to the Secret Service Protective Intelligence Division. Bob hoped to prove himself at ID, then present some of his protective intelligence ideas to supervisory agents. By no fault of his own, Bob was immediately enveloped in controversy. The Intelligence Division had wanted another agent transferred instead. Bob received a chilly reception from some, including the second-in-command.

Assigned to shift work at the ID duty desk, Bob worked hard and was a very able agent. He had much experience in PI investigations and operations. Given the task of updating the duty desk manual, Bob impressed the operations supervisor with the resulting product.

The 3:00 p.m.–11:00 p.m. shift was the most difficult for me. Bob would be gone before either our children or I arrived home from school; he'd come home after midnight. When I arose in the morning, he'd be sound asleep. With Bob working weekends as regular days, we spent little time together as a family.

In September 1979, Bob received commendations from two Secret Service Assistant Directors (AD) for the Service's overnight response to the explosion of a Titan II missile at Damascus, Arkansas. As coincidence would have it, Vice President Mondale was spending the night in the area, less than 50 miles away. Bob's alert action ensured the safety of the vice president.

Bob had also been rotated into the pool of agents assigned to out-of-town advances for President Carter and Vice President Mondale. Depending on the complexity of the visit and whether protectee overnights were involved, teams *usually* traveled three to four days in advance of vice presidential visits and four to five days in advance of the president.

President Carter's visit to Yugoslavia in June 1980 is remembered for the possibility that a foreign state secret had been divulged to Bob and Agent Dan Meyer, while conducting the ID advance.

When conducting an overseas advance, American law enforcement officers have no legal authority. They may only do what the host country allows. It is extremely important that advance team members establish friendly and effective liaison with their foreign counterparts.

It was the practice of ID advance agents to give their opposite numbers appreciation gifts. The gifts were presented at the first meeting, since there was usually no time to do so at the conclusion of the visit. It was also the belief of many that giving gifts upfront resulted in better cooperation.

After learning that their contact in the Yugoslav secret police liked fine Scotch whiskey, Bob and Dan purchased several large bottles of premium Scotch at the embassy commissary. Our boys presented the gift-wrapped bottles to the officer at their initial meeting. The Yugoslav colonel tore off the wrapping paper with the eagerness of a child opening birthday presents. When the Scotch was revealed, the colonel grasped our boys in a bear hug of gratitude and appreciation. Genuine Scotch whiskey was expensive and hard to come by within Yugoslavia.

The colonel seemed genuinely touched and invited Bob and Dan to be his guests for lunch. Later that day, the interpreter provided by the Ministry of the Interior took Bob and Dan about 10 miles south of Belgrade to Mount Avala. They would meet up with the colonel for lunch at a restaurant atop the mountain, accessible by a winding road through a forest of oak, beech, and pine.

At the summit, Bob and Dan paid their respect at the Monument to the Unknown Hero, which honors the soldiers who died fighting for Yugoslavia in World War I. They enjoyed a breathtaking view of the beautiful countryside and the city of Belgrade, which lies at the confluence of the Sava and Danube Rivers. They gazed at the nearby 666-foot-tall Avala TV tower. An architectural marvel, the tower was supported by a tripod of concrete legs, which stood upon the 1,700-foot-high mountain.

Next, Bob and Dan visited a memorial commemorating a deadly plane crash, which occurred on the western slope of Mt. Avala. The statue—designed in the shape of broken aircraft wings—was emotionally moving. On October 19, 1964, a Soviet Ilyushin-18 turboprop airliner slammed into Mt. Avala amid rain and fog and exploded in a fireball of death and destruction. The plane carried Marshal Sergei S. Biryuzov, Chief of Staff of the Soviet army, 6 other high-ranking Soviet officers, and 11 others. There were no survivors.

At the time of the crash, the aircraft was making an instrument approach to Surcin Airport, located eight miles west of Belgrade. The aircraft had wandered significantly off course and was at too low of an altitude to overfly the mountain. The Soviet military delegation had flown from Moscow to attend a celebration commemorating the 20th anniversary of the liberation of Belgrade during World War II.

While Bob and Dan were walking back from the memorial, they were met by the Yugoslav colonel, who was showing the effects of having imbibed too much of his new gifts. His movements were unsteady; rosy cheeks accented a broad smile. The colonel pointed to the monument in the distance and with slow, faltering speech made some remarks in his native Serbo-Croatian.

The interpreter looked bewildered by what he had just heard. "The colonel says he was part of the force that brought about the crash. He says they placed temporary radio beacons on the mountain and turned off the navigational equipment at the airport. That caused the Russians to home in on the mountain."

"He's telling us a story," Bob said to the interpreter in disbelief.

"I've been with the colonel for many years. I've never heard this before. I believe he's being truthful," stated the translator.

"Ask him why they would have done that," Bob inquired.

After the exchange of question and answer, the translator related: "The colonel says the Partisans [armed group opposing the Nazi occupation] liberated Yugoslavia, *not* the Russian army. The Russians invited themselves to the celebration. It was worried that the true purpose of their visit was to meddle in our affairs and threaten us with invasion."

"Isn't that something," remarked Dan Meyer.

Tragedy struck the Secret Service on January 14, 1980. Denver Field Office Special Agent Stewart Panson "Perry" Watkins was shot by Joseph Hugh Ryan, a former mental patient with a direction of interest toward U.S. presidents. Ryan was of record with the Secret Service dating back to 1974 when he showed up at the White House seeking to become an undercover narcotics agent. That visit earned Ryan a committal to St. Elizabeths Hospital.

Ryan had recently moved to the Denver area from Sacramento, California. He appeared at the USSS Denver Field Office complaining that he had been threatened by former President Nixon and was being harassed by the Secret Service. Since Denver agents were not familiar with the subject, a quick call was made to the ID duty desk.

The duty desk agent gave a synopsis of the subject's record, which included recent psychiatric treatment (1979). It was also noted that during a 1979 interview by Secret Service agents, the subject was found to be carrying a loaded .357 Magnum revolver, which was confiscated.

With that information, Denver agents asked if the subject was armed. Subject replied that he was. The interviewing agents kept an eye on the subject, while the Denver Police Department was called for assistance.

In the meantime, Agent Watkins entered the reception area. Ryan suddenly jumped to his feet and pulled a .45-caliber semiautomatic pistol from under his coat. Watkins grabbed for the weapon but was shot twice with hollow-point bullets. Watkins then pulled his revolver and fired one shot into Ryan before falling to the floor. With Watkins out of the line of fire, one of the interviewing agents shot Ryan four times to end the assault. Ryan died at the scene. Agent Perry Watkins died later that evening during surgery. It was a *very* bad day for the Secret Service.

Bob and I talked about the tragic event the following day. Suddenly, the abstract fear of Bob dealing with mental subjects hit home with lethal reality. A Secret Service agent had been shot dead by a PI subject. With the force of a tidal wave of emotion, a rush of anxiety engulfed me. Bob had dealt with PI subjects hundreds of times and continued to come in contact with them during Northwest Gate interviews and out-of-town advances.

"Was the agent married?" I asked.

"He had a wife and two teenage sons," Bob replied.

"Oh, no!" I cried out. I immediately felt a sense of the horror the agent's family must be going through. Tears fell from my eyes. I grabbed Bob and hugged him. "Bobbie, please be careful," I implored.

"Don't worry about me," Bob said. "I take every precaution to prevent this type of thing from happening. My job is to prevent anyone from having to become a hero. If it comes to that, then I've failed. And I don't intend on failing."

"Bobbie, what would you have done in this situation?"

"Actually, a *somewhat* similar situation happened to me several years back. A subject showed up at WFO wanting to speak with an agent. He said that voices told him to come to Washington *to make something big happen.* I scanned his body for bulges and didn't see any. I had another agent run his name through ID.

"The agent came back and slipped me a piece of paper with the results of the ID check hastily written on it. The subject was a former QI [Quarterly Investigation subject] from another district. He had been arrested several years before within a block of the president. At the time of the arrest, he was carrying a loaded .45 automatic. I still remember the note like it was yesterday. The words '.45 automatic' were in big letters and underlined.

"I nodded to the other agent in acknowledgement of the note and slid my right hand inside my suit jacket to grip my revolver. I then asked the subject if he was carrying a weapon. He answered no. Since he had been convicted of a gun violation in the past, I asked permission to conduct a 'pat down.' He agreed, and no weapons were found.

"If he had said he was armed, I would have drawn my weapon and ordered him to grab the wall. His admission to carrying a weapon would have been all I needed to disarm him. I don't know why that didn't happen in Denver, especially since the subject was paranoid and showed hostility to the Secret Service. It's always better if agents control the situation and not the subject. People carry things that they intend on using."

By his one-year anniversary at ID, the 1980 presidential campaign was in full swing. Because assassination attempts were so successful, Bob believed their prevention was paramount. He had thought long and hard on ways to prevent assassination. Bob called it *preventive* intelligence.

Since 1840, every president elected or re-elected in a year ending in zero had died in office. The chief reason Bob turned down other careers was to become a Secret Service agent and to help end this historical trend. Now, the time was at hand.

Bob approached his supervisor with several suggestions. One proposed that magnetometers (metal detectors) be used to screen guests at presidential events. Another suggestion was his PIER form to help determine the dangerousness of PI subjects.

He also advocated the use of telephone traps for presidential visits. With permission of the number's subscriber, the phone company could place a trap and trace on the line. This would decode the digital print of calling numbers for identification. Bob developed a permission form that he used in out-of-town advances. He found it extremely helpful in the investigation and prosecution of bomb and other telephonic threats.

Bob's recommendation for magnetometers was submitted through the employee suggestion program. It came back with a request that it be withdrawn. The Service did not want to broach the issue. It wasn't going to be approved, and the Service did not want to be second guessed if something happened.

Bob's PIER form was rejected by the ID supervisor who handled those matters. The supervisor did not see the need.

Bob's telephone trap form was adopted by the Service and still in use today. He received a commendation from the director along with a cash award.

In spite of the commendations, award, and superior evaluation by his immediate supervisor, Bob was unbelievably *passed over* for rotation off the duty desk. Bob was next in line, but the ID-SAIC overruled the reassignment. Bob spent an extra five months on the duty desk so that an agent the SAIC wanted to promote could gain some seasoning in a case control branch.

Time moved on. I asked Bob if anyone down at work ever mentioned the Presidential Curse. "No, and I'm not bringing it up. Otherwise, they'll send me to St. Elizabeths!"

Bob would soon know who the next president would be to face Chief Tecumseh's Curse.

Chapter 12

Rawhide

In the 1980 presidential election, former California Governor Ronald Reagan defeated President Jimmy Carter. Reagan's codename was "Rawhide," which reflected his starring roles in Hollywood westerns, his California ranch, and his love of horses.

Reagan rode into Washington to marshal in a new era. The theme for his inauguration was "A Great New Beginning." Secret Service Headquarters decided that Intelligence Division agents would conduct the PI advances for inaugural events attended by USSS protectees. Because of Bob's WFO experience, he was tapped to conduct the PI advance for the presidential inaugural gala that was held at the Capital Centre (demolished 2002) in Landover, Maryland.

The gala was billed as "The Beginning of a Great New Beginning." Over 18,000 guests filled The Capital Centre for a pre-inaugural celebration with President-elect Reagan, Vice-President-elect Bush, and their families. Johnny Carson emceed the event and stars performing included Frank Sinatra, Bob Hope, Charlton Heston, Debby Boone, Jimmy Stewart, Charley Pride, Rich Little, Donny and Marie Osmond, and others.

Inaugural balls were held at ten Washington locations: five hotels, three Smithsonian buildings, the Kennedy Center, and the Pension Building (now called the National Building Museum). Bob was given first choice as to which one he wanted to work on inaugural night. He immediately chose the Washington Hilton, while explaining, "There's an unsecured public area that borders the arrival and departure point. It's a potentially dangerous spot. The protective survey places the burden on the PI teams to cover the area."

For the Washington Hilton inaugural advance, Bob suggested that President Reagan wear his ballistic (bullet resistant) topcoat during the arrival and departure. The WFO lead advance agent asked if Bob had adverse intelligence. "No," Bob answered, "and if history holds true, we probably won't have any before the next assassination attempt. But, the T Street entrance to the hotel closely borders the arrival site. I'll have a PI team in the crowd, but it's a public area with a clear shot at POTUS [President of the United States]."

Bob added the warning to his intelligence situation report and thoroughly briefed his PI teams, who were from out-of-town and not familiar with the Washington Hilton. He directed one of the teams to devote most of the evening to the T Street entrance. He asked them to be in the area no later than 20 minutes before protectee arrivals and to remain there until the departures. "If you see anyone acting suspiciously or with bulges, check them out."

Bob then moved the stanchions for the rope line farther down the sidewalk, giving another couple of feet between the public and the president. As ID coordinator for the site, Bob handled ticket problems, inebriated guests, and like matters with inaugural staff and police. That freed up the PI teams to concern themselves with true protective concerns.

The visits by the Reagans and Bushes to the Washington Hilton were without incident. In fact, their visits to all ten inaugural sites were completed without any major problems.

Bob continued to work the ID duty desk. As luck would have it, he and two other agents were manning the duty desk for the day shift on Monday, March 30, 1981. Monday mornings were always busy as calls streamed into the Intelligence Division for the start of another work week. The morning hours passed quickly.

The president's schedule showed an afternoon movement to the Washington Hilton Hotel. He would be addressing the annual convention of the Building and Construction Trades Department of the AFL-CIO. Coincidentally, this group was one of the organizations that President Ford spoke to on September 22, 1975, before the assassination attempt by Sara Jane Moore.

As Reagan's departure time drew near, Bob selected USSS Charlie frequency on his workstation's radio in order to monitor the communications of the presidential detail. Bob also punched up the appropriate USPP and Metropolitan Police (MPD) radio channels.

Accompanied by Secretary of Labor Raymond Donovan, the president departed the South Grounds of the White House at 1:45 p.m. for the five-minute ride to the Washington Hilton. Shortly after 2:00 p.m., President Reagan addressed the 4,000 convention delegates. The mostly Democratic audience was polite but unenthusiastic about Reagan's economic program.

At the conclusion of the speech, the president exited the International Ballroom for his return to the motorcade area. At about 2:27 p.m., the site advance agent gave the signal that the president was coming out. About 10 seconds later, word came over both the USSS and police frequencies that gunfire had erupted and that there had been some injuries. On one of the police bands, Bob heard, "Shots fired; officer down!"

Bob immediately alerted the duty desk supervisor, Jim O'Neill, who had been busy with some paperwork. O'Neill glanced at the other duty agent, who confirmed the report with a nod of the head. Without saying a word, O'Neill headed for the office of Special Agent in Charge Richards.

In the meantime, PPD-SAIC Jerry Parr radioed: "Rawhide is okay, follow-up. Rawhide is okay." From the PPD follow-up vehicle (Halfback), supervisor Ray Shaddick asked Parr if they were going to the hospital or back to the White House. Parr notified that Stagecoach (the presidential limo) was en route back to Crown (the White House).

A sickening feeling came over Bob. He knew the Washington Hilton and its arrival/departure point all too well. Bob feared that his worst nightmare had become terrifying reality. Someone must have fired at President Reagan as he was leaving the hotel.

Even though SAIC Parr had relayed that the president was okay, Bob was still worried. A voice in the back of Bob's mind warned that the president might have been hit. The voice reminded Bob that bullet wounds can be hard to detect, especially if made by small-caliber ammunition. A bullet can pierce clothing—leaving only a small entry hole that may be overlooked. If the bullet stays in the body, there are no exit wounds. It's not like the movies; blood doesn't gush from entry wounds. However, the bullets can cause life-threatening internal bleeding.

Jim O'Neill returned with SAIC Richards. Both were relieved to hear that the president was apparently okay and on his way to the safety of the White House. Suddenly, Bob's nightmare took a frightening turn. The driver of the presidential limo (Agent Drew Unrue) notified the lead car agent (Mary Ann Gordon), "We want to go to the emergency room of George Washington." After Gordon acknowledged the message, Unrue added, "Go to George Washington fast!"

Bob hoped that the visit to the emergency room of George Washington University (GW) Hospital was just a precaution—to make sure the president hadn't been injured. Twenty seconds later, the change in destination took another ominous turn. Jerry Parr asked that a stretcher be ready on arrival. Halfback then asked the PPD command post W-16 (code name: Horsepower) if they copied that Stagecoach was now en route GW. Horsepower acknowledged that the hospital had been notified. Parr then radioed, "Let's hustle."

Had the Presidential Curse struck again? With the thought of the Secret Service losing another president to assassination too terrible to contemplate, Bob tried to reason other possibilities. Maybe Parr had been wounded. In the initial rush of adrenaline, Parr might not have realized he had been hit. Could it be that

Jerry Parr was being dropped off at GW for treatment? In any case, Bob said a silent prayer.

SA O'Neill divided the notifications to be made by the duty desk agents. Thus, within minutes of the shooting, the Intelligence Division began to notify all headquarters offices and divisions, all protective divisions, and the Washington Field Office of the incident. Those notified were responsible for passing the information within their respective divisions/offices and to take appropriate action as needed.

Although the president's condition and details of the incident were still uncertain, ID advised that shots had been fired during the president's departure from the Washington Hilton and that the presidential limo had expedited to GW Hospital. Duty desk personnel stated that updates would be forthcoming as soon as they were available.

It took Stagecoach less than four minutes to reach GW. Minutes later, PPD agents at the hospital confirmed Bob's fears. The president had indeed been shot. At first, it was believed that the president had escaped unharmed. SAIC Parr had valiantly covered the president and pushed him into the back of the presidential limousine at the first sounds of gunfire. Parr landed on top of Reagan with the president's chest striking the transmission hump.

As Stagecoach roared away from the Hilton and down Connecticut Avenue, Parr used his hands to probe Reagan for injuries. None were found. Soon, however, the president complained of chest pain and difficulty in breathing. In response to Parr's queries, Reagan responded that he didn't think he had been shot nor was he having a heart attack. Reagan believed a rib might have been broken when he was thrown into the limo.

Bringing a handkerchief to his lips, the president noticed some blood and thought he had cut his mouth. SAIC Parr observed that the bright red blood on Rawhide's lips was frothy. Parr recognized this as a sign of an injured lung. By now, Stagecoach was entering the tunnel under Dupont Circle. Parr was afraid Rawhide's lung had been punctured by a broken rib. Parr ordered Stagecoach to divert to GW. This decision *saved* the president's life.

Upon reaching GW Hospital, the president attempted to walk in under his own power but soon collapsed. He was carried into Trauma Bay 5, and his clothes were quickly cut away. Reagan's blood pressure was dangerously low. An intravenous (IV) drip was hooked up to the president and fluids began to flow. Blood was ordered. While the president was being rolled on his side, medical personnel observed a small slit under Reagan's left armpit. It was a gunshot wound!

Further examination revealed that the president's left lung had collapsed. The first objective of the emergency medical team was to raise Reagan's blood pressure to prevent him from going into shock. The president received oxygen. Next, a tube was inserted into the president's chest to drain blood in order to permit the damaged lung to re-expand. Reagan continued to receive fluids and blood was administered.

In the meantime, radio transmissions were overheard that a suspect in the shooting had been transported by Secret Service agents to MPD Central Cell Block. Bob wondered why the subject hadn't been taken to the USSS Washington Field Office for initial investigation until release to the FBI. Due to the events that occurred in Dallas after the 1963 assassination of John F. Kennedy, it had become a federal offense to assassinate, assault, or kidnap the president or vice president, or attempt to do so (18 U.S.C. 1751).

Lee Harvey Oswald had been shot and killed in the basement of the Dallas Police and Courts Building on live national television. With his death, it became impossible to close the case to the satisfaction of many. Conspiracy theories abounded and persist to this day. The investigative jurisdiction for violations of 18 U.S.C. 1751 was given to the FBI. The statute also gives federal investigation and prosecution *precedence* over state and local authorities.

One of the main responsibilities of a PI team after an assault on POTUS is to take action that would maintain an "interim federal presence." Until the FBI could take over, the crime scene needed to be preserved, witnesses detained, and a federal chain of custody begun. If an assailant or assailants were apprehended, they needed to be questioned as to the possibility of other co-conspirators. It was of prime importance to ascertain if a conspiracy existed and to what extent. Were others standing by to launch another assault on the president in case the first attempt failed or to attack the vice president and others in the line of presidential succession?

It didn't take long for the news of the assassination attempt to break over radio and television. After all, the White House Press pool had covered the ill-fated departure. It did take them about 45 minutes to find out that President Reagan had been taken to GWU Hospital for treatment. The media originally reported that the president had *not* been injured and had returned safely to the White House.

President Reagan spent approximately 40 minutes in the trauma area of the GW Emergency Room. During this time, a large amount of blood drained from the tube inserted into the president's chest. X-rays confirmed the presence of a bullet, possibly within Reagan's lung. With the president continuing to bleed internally, the decision was made to operate. SAIC Parr and PPD shift agents quickly donned surgical scrubs, so they could provide protection for the president during surgery.

The Intelligence Division swelled with the arrival of the 3-11 duty desk shift and with the addition of some headquarters personnel. The latter had responded to ID when it was activated as the USSS Command and Control Center. A major problem soon arose; it became almost impossible to obtain an outside telephone line. With news of the assassination attempt being spread far and wide, telephone circuits in downtown Washington were quickly overloaded.

It was even extremely difficult to obtain a White House signal line. The White House Communications Agency (WHCA) signal board had been swamped by heavy usage. Bob took the initiative and spoke with a WHCA supervisor. It was emphasized that ID was trying to determine if additional shooters and conspirators might exist. The WHCA supervisor promised to give ID priority. Bob made a similar call to the White House switchboard. Priority status was obtained for ID's White House extension.

An agent was dispatched to WFO in order to establish and to keep open a line between the field office and ID. The problem continued well into the evening. Dial tones were not readily available on commercial lines. This proved to be a major obstacle in receiving and passing on updated information. Had it not been for the WHCA signal board and the White House switchboard, the Intelligence Division would never have been able to be as effective as it was during the early hours of the incident.

ID was advised by the Washington Field Office of the identity of the shooting suspect. His name was John Warnock Hinckley Jr., a 25-year-old white male with addresses in Lubbock, Texas and Evergreen, Colorado.

After a short stay in a holding cell, the suspect was moved to the MPD Homicide Branch. With a USSS-SA looking on, an MPD homicide detective advised Hinckley of his rights and asked if he wanted to answer questions. Hinckley replied that he thought he should talk with an attorney first. The suspect did give some identifying data.

Around 5:00 p.m., Hinckley was turned over to the FBI. The U.S. Attorney's Office authorized the FBI to charge Hinckley for violations of 18 U.S.C. 1751 and 18 U.S.C. 111 (Assault on a Federal Officer). USSS-SA Tim McCarthy along with White House Press Secretary James Brady, and MPD Police Officer Thomas Delahanty were also wounded during the assault on the president.

Inside Operating Room 2, the president was anesthetized. Dr. Joseph Giordano then performed a "peritoneal lavage" to detect if the president's abdominal cavity had been injured. Giordano was concerned that the bullet or a fragment might have tracked through the abdomen. In addition, there was the danger that the president had been harmed when he was forcibly thrown into the limo. An incision was made and a saline solution rinsed about. The fluid was then drained and analyzed for the presence of blood. The test was negative.

Next, Dr. Benjamin Aaron opened up the president's chest in search of the bullet and the source of the bleeding. It took several hours to locate the bullet and to remove it. A bleeding artery was sutured back together. The president was wheeled to the recovery room at approximately 6:45 p.m. During the evening, the president's condition continued to stabilize. The word from the hospital was that the president would survive. It was great news!

John Hinckley was taken to the Washington Field Office of the FBI and again given a Miranda warning. A USSS agent sat in on the interview. Hinckley did not want to speak about the day's events until he could talk with his parents. He did answer questions regarding his travels, family, education, employment, medical history, and other general background information.

Hinckley divulged that he had received treatment from several mental health professionals. Most importantly, Hinckley identified a telephone number found in his wallet as one that connected to a Yale University dormitory. Hinckley said it was actress Jodie Foster's telephone number. Foster was enrolled at Yale, which is located in New Haven, Connecticut. Hinckley stated he had talked with the actress several times on the phone and that tapes of the calls were in a suitcase at his hotel room.

When Bob heard Jodie Foster's name mentioned, he excitedly turned to SAIC Richards and suggested, "This guy might be playing out the Travis Bickle role!" The blank look on Richard's face revealed that the reference was not understood. "The Travis Bickle character from *Taxi Driver*," Bob added. Richards still did not comprehend the meaning. Bob gave Richards a quick summary of the film and the significance of the roles played by Robert De Niro (Travis Bickle) and Jodie Foster (Iris). Richards then hurried off to relay the information to the supervisors who were in contact with WFO and the other USSS field offices that were monitoring FBI investigations in Denver, Lubbock, Dallas and elsewhere.

It now seemed more certain that Hinckley was a troubled individual, who had acted alone. Later that night, a search of Hinckley's D.C. hotel room confirmed the assessment. FBI agents with USSS agents assisting executed a search warrant at Room 312 of the Park Central Hotel, 705 18th Street, NW. It was ironic that the hotel was located only a block away from Secret Service Headquarters and often housed agents who were on temporary assignments to Washington.

The search revealed a note written by Hinckley an hour before he left for the Hilton. Addressed to Jodie Foster, the letter professed Hinckley's deep love for the actress and his desire to live out his life with her. Hinckley wrote that by shooting President Reagan, he hoped to gain Foster's respect and love.

Thus, the attempt on the life of the 40th president of the United States appeared to be an irrational scheme concocted to impress a young film actress and to live out a fantasy.

Chapter 13

3-31-81

As Bob drove to work on the morning after the Reagan assassination attempt, he reflected on what more could have been done to prevent the previous day's assault. A would-be assassin had exploited a weakness in Secret Service protection. Bob put a large amount of the blame squarely on his own shoulders. He was one of the agents who participated in the 1978 update of the Washington Hilton protective survey.

To accommodate the hotel's management, a potentially dangerous change was made to the survey. This created a breach in the 360-degree protective perimeter. Bob tried to have the decision reconsidered. A modification was made; a PI team was added to cover the exposed area, yet the breach remained. Now, guilt squeezed Bob's conscience like a steel vice. He should have done more he told himself, even if it would have significantly harmed his career. Bob should have listened to the warning from his inner voice. President Reagan came *very* close to dying.

Seeing the film, *The Tall Target*, stirred Bob's childhood fascination with presidential assassination and its prevention. In the film, Detective John Kennedy's warning of an assassination plot against Lincoln is ridiculed by Kennedy's superior. Kennedy has to resign from the force and take matters in his own hands. It was if the film had foreshadowed Bob's own plight.

Tecumseh's Curse haunted American history for 120 years (1840–1960). Bob joined the Secret Service and dedicated himself to breaking the curse for the president elected in 1980. By chance or fate, Bob had been on the survey team that almost cost this president his life. If Bob had shown the same resolve the Kennedy character did in *The Tall Target*, the assassination attempt on President Reagan would not have happened.

Uncanny thoughts continued to pass through Bob's brain as he walked from his Ellipse parking spot to USSS Headquarters. Bob's very *first* USSS protective assignment was at the T Street entrances to the Washington Hilton, where the assassination attempt had taken place.

My birthday was the same month and day (November 22) as the JFK assassination, and I was born in San Antonio, Texas, the first city visited by JFK in his ill-fated Texas trip.

Bob's initials, "RR," were the same as the president elected in 1980, Ronald Reagan, and also the same of author Robert Ripley, whose book had first inspired Bob (*Ripley's Believe It or Not!*). And all three men's first and last names contained exactly six letters each for a total of 12 per man!

Plus, Bob's and Reagan's first jobs were as lifeguards. And finally, Ronald Reagan starred in a series of Secret Service films as Agent Brass Bancroft

Had Bob been living in "The Twilight Zone"?

Bob took his place at the duty desk and reviewed the overnight developments. Further evidence of John Hinckley's irrational infatuation with Jodie Foster was revealed. It was also believed that Hinckley might have stalked Jimmy Carter. In fact, Hinckley had been arrested in Nashville, Tennessee on October 9, 1980, while attempting to board a commercial airliner. *Three* handguns were seized from Hinckley's suitcase. Hinckley paid a fine and was released. It was viewed as a routine arrest by local authorities and the FBI. The arrest information was not passed to the Secret Service even though President Carter was in Nashville conducting a "town meeting" on that date.

At about 8:45 a.m., Bob was called into SAIC Richards' office. Deputy Special Agent in Charge (DSAIC) Ron Claiborne was also present. "Bob, Tim Halfman mentioned that you had been concerned about the Hilton and had asked for that assignment for the inaugural—that it was a dangerous site," Richards queried.

"Yes, the protective survey was changed in 1978. Before that, the T Street entrance and that side of the block were closed down for arrivals and departures. What used to be a credentialed press area became a full-time public area," Bob stated. "The hotel complained that the temporary closures were too much of a hardship."

Both Richards and Claiborne were taken aback from what they had just heard; a momentary silence fell upon the room. "Bob, the director is worried," Richards said in an undertone. "There's already been press inquiries asking how Hinckley was able to get so close to the president. Questions have also been raised whether the area was a press area and about the positioning of the limo."

"A concrete island separates the VIP drop-off area from T Street," Bob explained. "After the arrival, they back up the limo, so it can pull straight out to T Street. That brings the limo and the president's departure path closer to the rope line. It also exposes the president for a longer period of time. Otherwise, the limo would have to pull forward from the VIP entrance and negotiate a very sharp turn and grade to connect with the hotel's main driveway and then out to Connecticut Avenue.

"Being that close to the rope line was never a problem when that side of the street was closed to the public," Bob continued. "It was a designated press area for arrivals and departures from the opening of the hotel in 1965 to the survey change of 1978. They still shepherd the press there for close-ups and that causes the confusion."

"Bob, we want you to interview the WFO-PI agents who worked yesterday's movement and also the squad's AT, Ed Dansereau. The director wants to know if there were any problems with the PI coverage."

"Sir, I don't know," Bob mused. "I don't have the grade to be reviewing the actions of others—especially a superior. Shouldn't Inspection be doing this?"

"Inspection is busy taking statements from everyone who worked the Hilton yesterday," Richards replied. "The director asked the ADs to conduct in-house investigations to find any problem areas. If mistakes were made, the director would rather get out in front of them before the congressional hearings. You know the drill for the Hilton; they won't be able to give you the runaround."

That evening, I anxiously bombarded Bob with questions regarding the assassination attempt and especially John Hinckley's motives.

"Hinckley identified with the Travis Bickle character from *Taxi Driver*," Bob related. "He was playing out the script with himself as lead. He bought guns and traveled around the country. He was obsessed with Jodie Foster and wanted to impress her. Hinckley thought the assassination of the president would win Foster's love. He also wanted to be somebody. He had been under psychiatric care, and the doctor advised Hinckley's parents to sever the ties to their son, so he could stand on his own. They said goodbye to him and cut off his money. John Hinckley Jr. became desperate. He was either going to live with Jodie Foster on Earth or live without her in heaven. Desperate people are dangerous people."

"So, are you a hero?" I asked.

"The heroes are Tim McCarthy, James Brady, Officer Delahanty, and Jerry Parr," Bob replied.

"I meant are you getting recognition for your opposition to the changes made at the Hilton. You were the only one who saw the danger and tried to do something about it."

Bob grimaced and answered with a terse, "No."

"Why not?" I asked in a disappointed tone.

"The higher-ups don't want that information to get out," Bob replied with some emotional agitation.

"What!" I blurted out.

"There's more; I was sent to WFO this morning to assess the PI coverage at the Washington Hilton," Bob related. "Two PI teams were originally assigned to the Hilton as *required* by the protective survey. One of the agents called in sick. Instead of finding a replacement or taking the assignment himself, the squad scheduler canceled one of the teams."

With anguish in his voice, Bob continued: "The remaining team didn't pick up the slack. They can be seen in the news video coming out of the VIP entrance only *a few short seconds* before the president. When I asked why they hadn't come outside in time to check the public area, the team's senior agent claimed that the president finished his speech early. 'What could we do?' he said.

"I told him he could have asked Jerry Parr to keep the president in the holding room until the area was checked and deemed safe. Jerry is one of the most easy-going supervisors ever.

"The truth is: Presidential movements within Washington have become routine. Some agents have grown complacent. Before yesterday, the last presidential assassination attempt in D.C. was in 1950. That's long before any of today's agents started their careers and before some were born. The agents work movement after movement in D.C.—day in and day out. For some, it becomes monotonous; the job takes on an unreal quality. Sooner or later, they're going through the motions on autopilot.

"Plus, WFO GS-14 supervisors never work sites, even presidential ones. So, there's really no one who can trouble-shoot deficiencies and take charge. Contrast that with out-of-town presidential visits where the district's SAIC and other supervisors cover every movement.

"And if there's no adverse intelligence, some agents let down even more. I go on the assumption that each and every movement is going to be the time that we're challenged. I prepare for the worst and look for ways to prevent it. I give it my all; you can't turn back the clock if something goes wrong. Yesterday should never have happened. It was taken for granted that the movement was going to be a *milk run*."

"That's not good."

"There's still more. I wrote up my findings and gave them to the administrative assistant of ID to be typed. She came to me later in the day and said she wanted to 'warn me.'"

"Warn you of what?" I asked.

"She's been around a long time. She started in the Chicago Field Office and worked there during the JFK assassination. She told me that 'funny things' went on back then and that she has the same feeling again."

"What kind of *funny things*?"

"I don't know; she wouldn't elaborate on that. She did say that SAIC Richards told her to type only an original of my report. No copies were to be made, not even the standard agent's copy. And she was ordered to shred my original handwritten submission! She knew how strange that was. She wanted to warn me to look out for myself."

"The Secret Service is playing you for a sucker," I said in anger. "You need to do something about this!"

"I did drop in to see Richards when I was pushed off the duty desk at the end of my shift. I asked for a copy of the report for my records. He got angry and ordered me not to mention anything about the report or what was in it ever again—*even to other agents*. When I started to protest, he told me to keep quiet, or I'd ruin my career."

"What are you going to do?" I asked.

"Nothing—what more can I do," answered Bob.

I filled with anger. Bob had given so much to the Secret Service. The sacrifices that he *and I* had made were superhuman. I had taken over all of the day-to-day family responsibilities. My professional and personal life had suffered. Bob had been a part-time husband and father for too long—*and for what*?

Some in the chain of command didn't care about anything but their own careers and the Secret Service's image. Bob had been a lone voice warning of the danger caused by the changes to the Hilton survey. Many visits had been made to the Washington Hilton since the changes of 1978. Yet, no one from PPD or WFO ever questioned them—except Bob. Now, Bob would be denied any recognition of his foresight, and his career was in jeopardy to boot.

Bob had been unfairly treated when he was passed over on the duty desk, but this latest episode was the epitome of raw deals.

Chapter 14

Aftermath

Finally, after 17 months of shift work on the ID duty desk, Bob was reassigned to the Intelligence Division's Liaison Branch to work with Agent Tim Halfman. Bob loved the position. Duties included keeping the SAICs and other high-level supervisors of PPD and VPPD briefed on the latest protective intelligence information. The branch also maintained intelligence liaison with the Uniformed Division (UD) and all other divisions and offices of the Secret Service in the D.C. area.

In addition, Tim and Bob were responsible for the evidentiary collection of any threat letters mailed to the White House. The letters were picked up from the White House Office of Correspondence. The letters were initialed, dated, placed in document protectors, and brought back to ID for investigation.

One of Bob's first initiatives as a liaison agent was to make the White House Northwest Gate interview room safer. He coordinated efforts to have the chairs in the room bolted to the floor, so they couldn't be used as improvised weapons. Other security enhancements were made and interview procedures updated.

Another important duty of the position was maintaining close liaison with the USSS freedom of information and privacy act officer. Requests to the Secret Service for disclosures under the Freedom of Information Act were searched through the various divisions and offices. For the Intelligence Division, Tim and Bob conducted the searches. When found, the records were reviewed and delivered to the freedom of information and privacy act officer for a determination of what could be released.

Plus, Bob became the ID contact for the Secret Service continuity of government (COG) officer. Bob was "read into" the program, which included the evacuation of the president, vice president, and other senior civilian leaders to safe relocation centers outside of Washington in times of national emergencies.

Bob also participated in nuclear/radiological exercises with the Nuclear Emergency Support Teams (NEST) of the Department of Energy. Field exercises were run with terrorist, extortionist, and post attack/nuclear accident scenarios. Bob marveled at some of the equipment utilized by the teams to include briefcase-size radiological detection devices.

After one of these exercises, the head of the White House Military Office, Edward Hickey Jr., invited Bob to lunch at the Navy Mess, located on the ground floor of the West Wing. Hickey was a former Secret Service agent, former State Department agent, and former director of the California State Police where he supervised Reagan's security during his years as governor.

"I want to thank you," Hickey said.

"For what?" Bob asked.

"Your alertness and quick action during the Arkansas missile explosion showed that the military office needed a shake-up. My position was created to provide coordination and direction. I owe you my job."

"No, problem," Bob responded. "Thanks for lunch."

"My pleasure. Maybe I can do more for you someday," Hickey replied.

Bob earned his keep in the Liaison Branch. In the weeks and months following the Reagan assassination attempt, the copycat phenomenon kicked in with a vengeance. Over a dozen subjects were arrested for making threats against President Reagan. Tim and Bob spent much time familiarizing themselves with active cases and passing the intelligence to SAIC Parr of PPD.

One case stood out in particular. This individual closely emulated John Hinckley Jr. The subject traveled to New Haven, Connecticut and watched Jodie Foster perform in a Yale University play. He sent a letter to Foster with the warning, "I will finish what Hinckley started." He also left a note in a New Haven hotel room that read, "I depart now for Washington, D.C., to bring completion to Hinckley's reality." Subject was arrested in a Manhattan bus terminal while attempting to board a bus for Washington. At the time of the arrest, he was carrying a loaded revolver.

In the fall of 1981, the world lost a champion of peace with the assassination of President Anwar Sadat of Egypt. The death of Sadat by extremists caused alarm and worry within the Reagan administration and among U.S. allies. Regimes in power in Syria, Iran, and Libya were hostile to Israel and the West. Libyan dictator Colonel Mu'ammar al-Qadhafi had a long history of troubled relations with the United States.

On October 9, 1981, NBC news broadcasted that President Reagan would not be attending Anwar Sadat's funeral due to a report that Colonel Qadhafi had ordered Reagan's assassination. It was alleged that the order for the assassination had been issued after an August incident in which two Libyan planes were shot down by the U.S. A USSS spokesperson denied the validity of the report. It was the first time a Libyan assassination plot targeting President Reagan appeared in the news. It wouldn't be the last.

In late November through December 1981, a number of news reports circulated that Qadhafi had dispatched a "hit squad" to the U.S. Targets listed were President Reagan, Vice President Bush, the secretaries of State and Defense, and White House aides. Some reports mentioned that two "death squads" had been sent. They were described as either five or seven members each. Several news dispatches stated the teams had already entered the U.S. Others cited the teams as poised to enter via Canada or Mexico. It was said that the assassination squads were armed with rocket-propelled grenades and surface-to-air missiles. Thus, both the presidential limo and *Air Force One* were in danger according to the media.

Anonymous intelligence and administration officials were cited as describing the original source of the information as a *credible informant*. When questioned by reporters about the plot, President Reagan advised that "the threat was real" and that "we have *complete* confidence in it." Colonel Qadhafi and the Libyan government denied the charges in the strongest of terms.

It was Bob's duty as a Liaison Branch agent to stay on top of the investigations surrounding the so-called "Libyan hit teams" and to keep the SAICs of PPD/VPPD and UD senior officials updated on the latest revelations. For his part, Bob was privy to and had knowledge of all information regarding the alleged assassination teams. Bob was on board from the very beginning.

Bob told me that he believed the entire affair was taking on a "life of its own" and being *politicized*. I have firsthand knowledge of some of this. Our phone rang at about 4:00 a.m. one morning in early 1982. It was the ID duty desk asking Bob to come in as soon as possible. Upon arrival, Bob was anxiously told by the duty desk supervisor, "A Libyan hit team is in the Washington area!"

Bob reviewed the information that had come in overnight. The previous evening, a radio hobbyist had overheard some strange transmissions, while operating a newly purchased scanner at his home, located near the George Washington Memorial Parkway and Washington National Airport. The transmissions were being sent over the Citizens Band (CB) with an alteration in the frequency, so standard CB radios would not be able to hear what was being said. With "Libyan hit teams" all over the news and the conversations sounding like a Middle Eastern dialect, the hobbyist recorded the transmissions and rushed them to the Department of State in D.C. There, an interpreter translated the conversations as at least three different individuals checking positions and distances.

When the intelligence alphabet agencies (CIA, FBI, and NSA) got hold of this, it was feared that a Libyan hit team had arrived and that it was triangulating positions for a motorcade attack. Of course, questions were raised as to what other locations the assassination team might have checked and when they would strike.

WFO, W-16, the Vice Presidential Protective Division (VPPD) command post, the UD command post, other protective details, and headquarters officials were notified by USSS-ID. The SAICs of both PPD and VPPD or their representative were asked to come in early in order to receive a special briefing from Bob. Assassination fervor swept through the Secret Service like a desert sand storm.

Fred Mann, the agent from the Foreign Intelligence Branch, arrived. He had been called in to prepare a teletype for transmittal to area law enforcement agencies. When Mann heard the news, he acted as if he had just won the lottery. Displaying a broad smile, he beamed with joy. He had consistently evaluated the Libyan hit team threat as real and this news was the validation he had hoped for. "They're here!" he excitedly told Bob.

Bob thought another explanation might be more likely. Fred and Bob headed for the USSS Technical Security Division (TSD) where they listened to a copy of the tape. They were told that the radios had been specifically tuned to the same nonstandard frequency for privacy. "This couldn't have happened on its own," the TSD specialist remarked. "It must be a Libyan hit team."

"Yes," Mann eagerly agreed.

To Bob, the transmissions sounded like they originated from *moving* vehicles. If the subjects were triangulating firing positions, Bob reasoned that they would have been stationary.

"Guys," Bob said, "I think I know what this is. There are a lot of gypsy cab drivers operating in Northern Virginia. Many are here illegally; most don't have hack licenses. I know from my experience as a former U.S. Park Police officer that they secretly communicate with each other via Citizen Band radios. They cruise about looking for fares and keep each other informed as to their location. They try to stay clear of the police and hide their activities." Mann looked at Bob as if he had just shot down Santa's sleigh.

TSD passed Bob's information to the State Department. With this new outlook and a different interpreter, it was discovered that the subjects were reporting their locations to each other and where they had found *passengers*. It was confirmed that Bob's hypothesis was correct. A cadre of gypsy cab drivers had been mistaken for a Libyan assassination squad.

Bob walked over to the Executive Office Building and passed the information to Jerry Parr, who had a good laugh over the false alarm. At the EOB offices of the Vice Presidential Protective Division, Bob informed the supervisor on duty, Frank Brown, of the resolution of the overnight scare. Brown was no stranger to Bob. Some years before, Brown had tried to have Bob unjustly disciplined. The action resulted from Bob's reluctance to hand *classified* national security information to foreign nationals.

Brown looked solemnly at Bob. "We still have to be vigilant. The teams are out there—somewhere," Brown stated with conviction.

"The information has to be taken seriously—for sure. I wouldn't put anything pass Qadhafi," Bob agreed. "He's a murderous dictator. The Service and the FBI are leaving no stone unturned, but so far we haven't been able to corroborate the key details of the informant's story."

"We're hearing a different tune over here," Brown declared. "Staffers are telling us that the information has been confirmed and is reliable."

"Staff people and national security types are not criminal investigators, and I think that's where the confusion begins," Bob remarked. "They have a layman's knowledge and understanding of criminal investigations. Because polygraph examinations of the source showed no deception or were inconclusive, the non-law enforcement types immediately took that as corroboration and evaluated the information and informant as reliable. We as criminal investigators can't do that—especially with a new informant who has no track record of reliability. That's against federal procedures.

"When you also consider that the source demanded a large sum of money *upfront* and that many foreign cultures don't have a stigma about lying, the informant's story and polygraph results should be questioned even more."

"They're pretty sure this is the real deal," Brown asserted. "Maybe they have access to more of the intelligence."

"I've read every piece of information on this," Bob replied. "There's no hard evidence that this informant's story is true. We've been checking every possible angle. I and other ID agents have volunteered [no pay] a lot of off-duty time reviewing tens of thousands of Customs declarations and Immigration forms. Other indices have been checked too. The informant supposedly prepared false identification documents for team members. We haven't had one worthwhile hit on any of the names we've been given.

"Frank, you're welcome to drop by ID and review the files for yourself. I'll be happy to set it up for you."

"No, that won't be necessary," Brown replied.

Returning to ID, Bob spoke with DSAIC Ron Claiborne. "Ron, I just got back from VPPD. They've been told by staffers that the Reagan hit team information is reliable and credible. Intelligence, administration, and sources on Capitol Hill have also been reported as confirming the existence of the teams. Even President Reagan has publicly expressed confidence in the information. With the Secret Service taking the lead in the domestic part of the current investigation, I'm concerned there may be some fallout on us. We haven't *corroborated* the informant's story."

"Don't worry about it," Claiborne snapped. "Richards and I have attended National Security Council meetings on this.

They're happy with what they've been hearing. If they're reading more into it than there is, it's a win for us. The Reagan assassination attempt and Libyan death squads are the justification we need for more money and agents. The Service is submitting a budget request for an additional shift for PPD, so they can be routinely rotated through assault on the principal [AOP] exercises and other in-service training. We've also been asking for funds for counter assault teams [CAT] and magnetometer screening. And UD [Uniform Division] wants funding to make the Ellipse patrol car permanent."

As the weeks went by without any trace of the hit teams, initial reports were questioned by the press, Congress, and the public. Eventually, it was suggested by diehards that the assassination squads had been recalled due to the uncovering of the plot. No detailed information supporting the existence of the Reagan hit teams was ever released by U.S. authorities.

In April 1982, Bob graduated from a two-week "Questioned Document Course" put on by the Secret Service. Always wanting to gain more knowledge and to better himself, Bob learned the basics of handwriting analysis. By obtaining and comparing known writing with disputed writing, Bob could help determine the authorship of various questioned documents. This was extremely helpful in Secret Service investigations involving forgery and in intelligence cases dealing with threatening letters. Bob studied techniques for breaking down writing into individual characteristics that showed differences and similarities in compared writings.

It didn't take long for Bob to put his new knowledge to use. He was transferred to the Analysis and Control Branch of ID. Bob took over the GS-12 agent position in Region IV, assisting his friend Chuck Krall, who was the 13. Region IV handled the Western field offices.

Bob meshed smoothly into his new assignment and became a valuable asset in the referral and review of intelligence cases. Chuck Krall handed Bob one case, asking him to write it up for submission to the Behavioral Science Unit (BSU) of the FBI for their evaluation and assistance. "Put your gloves on," Krall joked. "This one's *really* cold." At the time, it was the oldest unsolved threat case in Secret Service files.

The case dated back to the mid-1960s when President Lyndon Johnson received threatening letters from an anonymous writer. The unknown subject was coined "The Traveler" by the Secret Service because the letters were mailed from different locations across America. Since some of the locations were places where LBJ had visited, it was believed the subject was stalking the president. The subject was evaluated as presenting a danger to President Johnson.

Through the years, investigation failed to determine the identity of the writer. The individual continued to mail in threats directed against the presidents who succeeded Johnson: Nixon, Ford, Carter, and Reagan. Even though it became apparent that the subject was more interested in blowing off steam than burning up gunpowder, the individual had committed numerous federal felonies and had been a long-time nemesis to the Secret Service.

It took two large file folders to hold all the paperwork that had been generated in the case. The two folders stacked about eight inches high. "Chuck, let me go through these first to see if I can find some investigative leads we can explore," Bob requested. "I'd like a shot at it before sending it off to the Bureau."

"Okay, Bob, you got it," Krall agreed.

Bob had done his own profiling when he worked PI at WFO. Although he had the highest respect for the Bureau and its BSU, Bob felt confident he could produce a psychological profile just as meaningful. Drawing upon his experience in threat assessment, Bob reviewed the many threatening letters and pages of reports before him. Bob stayed late that evening until a picture of the anonymous writer came to mind. Bob saw an aging white male who jumped around from town to town and job to job. The subject had no pension plan and was just eking out an existence. He would be dependent on Social Security for a lifeline in his later years. The subject had opinions about everything, and Social Security would be no exception. The subject was angry at the cards he had been dealt. Threats made him feel powerful, and he gained some revenge. The subject enjoyed knowing the Secret Service was jumping through his hoops. He saw this as a game he was continually winning, and it added to his feeling of superiority.

It was time for pay back. Bob wrote a referral for the field office in the city where one of the latest threatening letters had been postmarked. Bob noted several distinguishing individual characteristics found in the unknown subject's writings. He requested that the field office show a copy of the unknown subject's latest handwritten letter to the local Social Security office as well as other governmental offices covered by the originating zip code. Bob believed it was likely that the individual had written "complaint type" letters to other authorities.

The next afternoon, Bob was coming back to his desk from a late lunch. Chuck Krall greeted Bob with a broad smile. "Bob, guess who just called and was saying good things about you?"

"Director Simpson," Bob replied facetiously.

"Danny Gibson called. They caught 'The Traveler.'"

"For real," Bob replied.

"Yeah, they arrested him this morning," Krall confirmed. "They took the letter to the Social Security office. The office manager took one look at it and said, 'That's Melvin Griggs.'

"They get Griggs' address and take a run out to his apartment. Griggs opens the door and Gibson identifies himself. Griggs says, 'How did you find me? After all these years, I didn't think I'd ever get caught!'

"Nice job, Bob. Gibson wanted me to pass his compliments to you. He said several times, 'This is the way ID should work.'"

Later that afternoon, Chuck Krall told Bob that he was wanted in SAIC Thomas' office. Thomas was in his first week as SAIC of the Intelligence Division. He had replaced former SAIC Richards, who moved into a deputy assistant director position at headquarters.

"Bob, I think Thomas may want to commend you," Chuck said. "You brought to justice a violator who we've been after for almost 20 years." Bob smiled at Chuck and hoped he was right. It was good timing that Bob would crack a decades old case with a new SAIC on board. Maybe Bob's luck was about to change. Richards certainly hadn't helped Bob's career; maybe it would be different with the new SAIC.

Bob knocked on the half-open door to SAIC Thomas' office. "Yes," answered a voice from within.

Bob peeked his head through the opening; "Sir, I'm Bob Ritter; you wanted to see me."

"Yes, come in." Bob entered the office and stood before the SAIC. Thomas stated in a monotone, "Give me your dream field office, and I'll do my best to get you there."

Thoroughly astonished, Bob replied, "Sir, I don't understand."

"Well, I thought you would from what I just heard," remarked Thomas with some surprise. "I just got an earful from SAIC Wilson of VPPD about you being burned out. We need to get you out of headquarters and back to the field."

"Sir, I don't know what you're talking about."

"I got a complaint that your work in and out of D.C. has been *less than desired*. Burnout happens to the best of us. It's nothing to be ashamed of."

"I've had superior evaluations and commendations. Any suggestion that I haven't been doing a professional job is news to me. I strongly refute the charge and ask for a chance to defend myself; there's two sides to every story," Bob asserted. "I like it in Region IV."

Thomas thought for a moment. "Since you want to stay in ID, I'll look into this further. In the meantime, decide which field office you'd like to transfer to. It can be Honolulu, San Diego, Miami, or wherever. Tomorrow, I'll let you know what I find out and my decision."

"Sir, when I leave D.C., I want to go to an RA [Resident Agency]. I don't want to go to a field office," Bob said.

"That's not going to be an option. This would need to be a quick transfer. Once you get to a field office, then you can work on an RA," Thomas advised.

"Things have been going on here that you don't know about," Bob stated. "I'm not going down without a fight."

"Let me look into this first," Thomas said. "We'll talk more tomorrow."

Bob came home that night, and he was as low as I have ever seen him. I felt sorry for Bob and for us. I couldn't help but think about the time Bob had turned down a position in a picturesque Western resident agency due to my reluctance to move during the school year. It turned out to be a big mistake.

"What are you going to do?" I asked.

"I'm going to fight it. There's no basis to the charge. This is *character* assassination," Bob replied with anger in his voice.

"Which field office are you going to choose?"

Bob thought for a while then answered, "I'm hoping it doesn't come to that."

The next morning, Bob was called back to SAIC Thomas' office. Moving boxes were still stacked in the corner; the walls were bare. Thomas still hadn't found time to unpack.

"Bob, I really have no choice," Thomas began somewhat apologetically. "Even though I found a whole lot of nothing, SAIC Wilson thinks you're burned out. I can't have someone here that I can't assign to VP advances. Give me your top field office, and I'll make the call."

"Sir, this isn't fair. What are the specifics? I should have the right to defend myself," Bob asserted.

"They claimed you didn't take the Libyan hit teams seriously—that you had a cavalier attitude. They specifically mentioned that your performance during the VP's visit to Denver was troublesome.

"My call to Denver didn't find any evidence of that," Thomas continued. "SAIC Griffiths [Denver Field Office] said his two PI agents and the local police related that you did an excellent job. He added that no one from the VP detail made any complaints to him. In fact, they told him everything went fine. Griffiths said you're welcome back in his district anytime. I mentioned this to Wilson, but the bottom line is *they've* lost confidence in you."

"This is unfounded," Bob stated. "Frank Brown might be behind this. He was one of the VP supervisors for the Denver trip. He tried to have me unfairly disciplined some years ago."

"That may be, but I can't let this become a distraction for ID. You've been here three years. I made my decision. It'll be best for you to move on with your career. Bob, *you're not going to be promoted here.*"

The last comment was the coup de grace for Bob's ID career. Bob would not be recommended for promotion. Bob's superior work, sacrifices, and successes flashed by in an instant—all for naught. The only thing left was his good name, and he didn't want to lose that. "I'm going to fight this," Bob said with stern conviction.

"You don't have grounds for that," Thomas said. "This is *not* a disciplinary action. It's a routine career transfer. Nothing's going in your file.

"From what I've seen, you've done a good job here and that's what I'm telling your next SAIC. Which field office do you want to go to?"

"WFO," Bob replied.

"Okay, you got me on that one. I did tell you *any* field office. The intent was to get you away from Washington. I didn't think WFO would be in your dream list."

"I didn't think so either," Bob responded.

"I'll make the call today," Thomas promised.

Chapter 15

A New Beginning

Bob said he picked WFO, so we wouldn't have to relocate. We could wait for an opening at a resident agency without having to make an extra move. And Bob intended on fighting the smear campaign that had been leveled against him. It would be easier to seek redress while still in the Washington area.

Bob had conducted 43 out-of-town advances (mostly presidential) while assigned to ID. He had received superlative comments in a good number of these. He had performed admirably in all his assignments, including an *extra* five months on the duty desk. With commendations, a director's award, and excellent evaluations in Bob's personnel file, the events of the last 24 hours were almost unbelievable.

Looking back on the Denver advance, Bob remembered a brief conversation with Frank Brown as the vice presidential party was boarding *Air Force Two*. While Bob and his Denver Police Department PI counterpart, a detective sergeant, were standing on the tarmac, Brown approached them and asked, "Why wasn't that PI subject removed from the motorcade area?"

"Frank," Bob answered calmly, "she wasn't a PI subject; she was a bag lady, well-known to the local PD. She was checked out. She was in the next block up from the hotel and presented no problem to the VP."

"We don't roust the homeless in this city," the detective sergeant added. "The press and the ACLU would have had a field day."

Brown looked at the detective and commented, "I didn't want you to move her." Pointing to Bob, Brown continued, "I wanted him to." Brown then turned and boarded *Air Force Two*.

Bob quickly forgot the exchange, but it now appeared that Brown must have lodged a complaint with the SAIC of VPPD. Bob knew he had made the right decision. The original radio message from Brown stated that a "staffer" had reported seeing a PI subject. Homeless persons are not PI subjects. People living on the streets of cities are a fact of American life. They may be an *embarrassment* to politicians, but they pose no physical threat. If they're not breaking the law and their behavior doesn't present a danger to themselves or others, law enforcement officers have no legal authority to move them against their will.

Homeless persons; lawful, peaceful demonstrators; non-dangerous mental subjects; and the like have civil rights just like everyone else in our society. The Secret Service has no legal justification to forcibly remove citizens who are lawfully exercising their constitutional rights. That's what makes us different from most countries in the world. Bob and every other Secret Service agent took an oath to *support and defend* the Constitution of the United States. Bob took his oath seriously.

Bob also knew that the potential danger for the vice president laid in the crowd that had assembled for his departure. Plus, nearby windows and rooftops could become sniper nests. If Bob and the police detective had been tied up running off a bag lady, they wouldn't have been able to cover the departure. That lesson should have been learned from the Reagan assassination attempt. Since no mistakes were admitted to by the Secret Service, its protective intelligence culture didn't change. PI teams continued to be looked upon as primarily a reactive asset.

It didn't take long for Bob's transfer. He finished up at ID that Friday and reported to WFO on the following Monday morning. Assigned to the Criminal Squad, Bob shared a two-man office

with his long-time friend Dick Corrigan. Bob still had good police contacts in the area and made a smooth transition back to
the street. It was just like the old days.

Bob got off to a great start. He solved some major cases and
led not only the squad but also the office in monthly arrests.
One case involved a Uniformed Division officer who discharged
his gun while on duty. The officer claimed a subject had tried to
run him over with a motor vehicle. The officer fired at the vehicle in self-defense. This occurred on a midnight shift, and some
USSS supervisors suspected that the officer had accidentally
fired his weapon and invented a "phantom car" assault for a
cover story.

Bob interviewed the UD officer, and a reenactment was conducted at the scene of the crime, a foreign mission located in
upper Northwest D.C. The officer stated he was on foot patrol
when he observed a vehicle circling the neighborhood. When
the officer stepped into the street to stop the suspicious vehicle
for a check, the driver sped up and drove right at the officer. The
officer dove out of the way while pulling his service revolver and
discharging it at the vehicle.

The automobile was occupied by two subjects in their early
20s—a male driver and a female passenger. The officer believed
the female cried out "Gil" during the incident. The officer described the vehicle as an older model two-door with Virginia
tags.

Bob thought "Gil" was most likely the driver's nickname. Bob
ran the name along with "Gilbert" through Northern Virginia
police departments and through the Virginia Department of
Motor Vehicles. Over a dozen possible suspects were discovered
in the region. Bob systematically eliminated each one until he
struck pay dirt.

Gilbert "Gil" Payne was a 22-year-old, who resided in Fairfax
County, Virginia. Investigation revealed the name of Payne's
girlfriend. Under interrogation, the suspect's girlfriend admitted that she was the female passenger during the incident in
question. She stated that Payne had been drinking and had "lost

his head." Fearing that the officer had gotten the tag number, Payne left the vehicle at a friend's residence in Arlington, Virginia. The subject then left town for places unknown.

Bob recovered the subject's vehicle, which had a bullet hole in the right-rear quarter panel. With the physical evidence and the sworn statement of the girlfriend, Bob submitted a criminal complaint to a U.S. magistrate. An arrest warrant was issued. From toll records of calls placed to Payne's girlfriend, Bob ascertained a Miami telephone number. The number was listed to a pay phone outside a Miami eatery.

Bob sent a collateral investigation to the Miami Field Office (MFO). MFO agents responded to the restaurant and discovered that Payne was working there as a waiter. He was arrested and taken before a federal magistrate. The defendant waived extradition, and the U.S. Marshals Service transported him back to D.C. for trial. Payne subsequently pled guilty to assault charges. For his effort, Bob received commendations from a USSS Assistant Inspector and the Assistant Director for Inspection.

In another high-profile case, Bob investigated the theft of an agent's service revolver. The agent claimed that the weapon was stolen from the glove box of his POV, while it was parked at his residence. Again, there was suspicion of misconduct. Bob received a call from one headquarters official who advised: "Give this one a good toss. This guy could have gotten rolled in a bar or something. The story as to how his gun was stolen might be fiction.

"I want to emphasize to you how important it is that you recover the weapon and sooner than later," the official continued. "We don't need a Secret Service handgun being used in the commission of a robbery or murder."

"I'll keep working until I find it," Bob assured.

An interview of the agent whose gun was missing did not generate any leads. The agent had no idea who might have taken the weapon. Bob believed the agent was telling the truth as to the circumstances of the theft.

A check with local police revealed that the community where the agent resided had been previously free of burglaries and car break-ins. Next, Bob canvassed the agent's neighborhood. He developed the names of several young teenagers who had been suspected by one resident of committing juvenile pranks such as painting graffiti.

On a hunch, Bob decided to interview these subjects. In the presence of their parents, the juveniles admitted to stealing the revolver. They knew the vehicle was owned by a Secret Service agent and decided to go through the car's interior. They were surprised to find a loaded firearm in the glove box.

The juveniles took the weapon to a local gravel pit where they fired off a shot. The kick and sound generated from a Treasury Department high-velocity round fired through the short barrel revolver were too much for our young desperados. As they were returning home, the juveniles scattered the remaining five rounds through a wooded area. One of the subjects retained the pistol, hiding it in his bedroom closet.

Within two days of the reported theft, Bob had recovered the weapon and four of the rounds tossed in the woods. The fifth round was never found, even after many hours of searching by Bob and an EOD team utilizing a mine detector.

In lieu of federal prosecution, the teenagers pled guilty in state juvenile court to larceny charges. The agent whose duty weapon was recovered dropped by WFO to thank Bob. The agent was happy his name had been cleared. The agent knew supervisors had speculated he had lost the weapon under unsavory circumstances.

Although Bob enjoyed working criminal cases, he was still upset over having been unfairly forced to vacate his Region IV position in ID. Bob had also been made an unwilling part of the USSS coverup regarding the missteps leading to the Reagan assassination attempt. While the Secret Service could claim that it had saved the president's life, it was responsible for putting him at risk in the first place.

For advice, Bob chatted with an attorney, whom Bob had known since his Park Police days. The attorney wanted to file suit against the Secret Service seeking either Bob's return to the Intelligence Division or his transfer to a resident agency. Counsel would argue that SAIC Thomas' decision was derived arbitrarily and that the charges laid against Bob were unjust and fueled by a supervisor who may have been seeking retribution. Additional claim would be made that Bob's knowledge of the Reagan attempt coverup and of the hype spun regarding the "Libyan hit teams" contributed to the situation.

The attorney made it clear that he needed to introduce the latter evidence to bolster Bob's case. After all, Bob had been warned that his career would be in jeopardy if he disclosed the truth about the assassination attempt. The attorney would represent that Bob's hasty departure from ID might have been a preemptive strike against a potential whistle-blower. It was significant that the original intent of the field transfer was to get Bob out of D.C. without delay. The new SAIC of ID folded on Bob fairly quickly. What part did former SAIC Richards and DSAIC Claiborne have in the decision, if any?

Bob considered his options. He knew information damaging to the Secret Service would be made public if the case went to trial. There was a strong probability that these revelations might lead to a Congressional hearing. The whole matter might become embroiled in partisan politics. Who knows what harm might come to the Secret Service? Bob could win the battle but lose the war. Many of his fellow agents would see Bob as a traitor.

Six months went by; Bob couldn't bring himself to filing suit. Instead, he continued to rack up arrests and convictions. Fiercely loyal to the Secret Service, Bob changed his strategy. He would stay in WFO and strive for a promotion to a GS-13. Many more resident agent positions are available for 13s than 12s.

There was one major problem with the plan; Bob couldn't shake the feeling that he was responsible for the president's near assassination and for the tragedy that struck down White House Press Secretary James Brady. Since 3-30-81, Bob's remorse at not having done more to prevent the Hilton arrival/departure point from being opened to the public became overwhelming.

If President Reagan had died, the truth would have come out. National mourning would have turned to national anger. Losing two popular presidents within 20 years would have been a deathblow to the protective mission of the USSS. In all probability, the Secret Service would have been stripped of its protective duties.

With the president's narrow escape from death and his rapid recovery, Secret Service management seized the opportunity and turned near failure into success. Treasury and USSS officials stated that no clear security mistakes were made. Although the Secret Service rationalized away wrongdoing, it quietly took steps to prevent a similar tragedy. A magnetometer screening program was instituted for the White House and for presidential visits. And at the Washington Hilton, a tent-like structure was used to enclose the presidential limousine and VIP entrance during arrivals and departures. No longer would presidential arrivals/departures be in plain sight of the public. It took the near assassination of President Reagan for the Secret Service to finally move forward.

These were needed and welcomed changes, but lost in all of the heroics of saving the president's life was the "Devastator" bullet that exploded deep inside Jim Brady's brain. Brady nearly lost his life. What was left of it was severely handicapped. Brady spent eight months in GWU Hospital. He experienced multiple major surgeries and developed infections, pneumonia, seizures, convulsions, and memory loss. Brady underwent grueling physical therapy, yet remained paralyzed on his left side. Unable to perform many everyday activities, he spent much of his time in a wheel chair. Brady's future looked bleak.

Bob knew he could have prevented the tragedy. Bob continued to fault himself for not doing more in 1978 to have the Washington Hilton survey changed. He should have aggressively challenged USSS culture. The opening of the T Street entrance area to the public during arrivals and departures was a *major* mistake, plain and simple. It almost cost two people their lives, one of them the leader of the free world. Not only did the survey change provide an easy opportunity for an assassin, it also helped to prompt the assassination attempt in Bob's estimation.

Would-be assassins like Arthur Bremer, Sara Jane Moore, and John Hinckley Jr. view lax Secret Service security as a call to action. It reinforces their delusions and compulsions and psychologically empowers them to seize the moment. It's the final piece of the puzzle that locks in their destiny and fate, the grand opportunity they've been waiting for to achieve their fantasies and their place in history.

On March 30, 1981, John Hinckley Jr. waited outside the Hilton Hotel for the departure of the president. Carrying a loaded handgun in his pocket, Hinckley could hardly believe his luck. No one from the Secret Service paid any attention to him. There were no agents inside the public area scrutinizing the crowd—as the protective survey called for.

Suddenly, President Reagan exited the hotel for the presidential limousine. The repositioning of the limo caused Reagan to come within 15 feet of Hinckley. At this close range, Reagan looked larger than life. The president waved to the crowd; Hinckley believed the gesture was meant for him alone. It was the affirmation of Hinckley's starring role. With the stage set, Hinckley's distorted mind started to roll. A voice from within cried out *action*. Hinckley pulled his weapon and fired it at the president. The president and three others were hit. President Reagan and Secretary Brady barely escaped with their lives. James Brady was permanently injured. It was all too easy—and all preventable.

If Bob had worked PI at the Hilton that day, *it never would have happened*—even with a flawed survey. Hinckley would have been found out and arrested. Or seeing the heightened security, he would have fled the area as Travis Bickle did in *Taxi Driver*. Of this, *I'm certain.*

Bob tried to get over his guilt, but he couldn't. Maybe senior executives of the Secret Service could live with the omission of the truth, but Bob couldn't. Maybe others could feel no responsibility for James Brady's tragic outcome, but Bob couldn't. No one was harder on Bob than Bob. He needed closure.

Bob came home one night and announced that he had given two weeks' notice to the Secret Service. I was at a loss for words. I never saw it coming. Bob informed me that he was transferring to the Department of Health and Human Services (HHS), Office of the Inspector General (OIG).

Former Secret Service Agent Charles "Charlie" Maddox was the Director of the Security and Protection Division at HHS. Maddox needed a qualified and experienced agent to assist in the protection of the secretary of HHS. Besides providing personal protection for the secretary, the position would entail the establishment of professional procedures, the writing of protective manuals, and the everyday coordination of the protective effort. It would be a new beginning for Bob and get his mind off the Secret Service demons that haunted him. Bob needed a *lifeline.*

I honestly didn't think it would happen. He was totally dedicated to the Service, and I couldn't see him leaving voluntarily. In his second tour at WFO, Bob was a well-respected agent, who was performing superlatively. He had worked hard during his Secret Service career. Both of us had sacrificed and had persevered for the Secret Service; it had become a big part of our existence.

As the days passed, Bob said little about the coming transfer. On the evening before his scheduled last day, Bob looked very apprehensive. I knew what was troubling him. "Are you really going through with it?" I asked.

"I don't know, Jan," Bob answered. "Tomorrow will tell."

"Bobbie, what about the Presidential Curse?"

"The curse has been *broken*," Bob answered. "The Secret Service has finally come of age."

After dinner, Bob went into the living room and cued up Vince Guaraldi's "Cast Your Fate to the Wind" on our stereo's turntable. He played the tune many times in a row. Each time, Bob closed his eyes and relaxed to the song's beautiful melody. He appeared to be deep in thought. The imagery of the song was not lost on me.

The following morning, I sent Bob off with a hug and a kiss and told him that whatever he decided would be fine with me. I fully believed that Bob would change his mind and stay with the Secret Service. I knew better than anyone else what the USSS meant to Bob.

I was truly surprised when Bob called me at school that afternoon and asked to be picked up at the Metro subway station. I knew then that Bob had done it. He had signed the papers, turned in his equipment, and dropped off the government car. As I drove Bob home, I remarked with some astonishment and disbelief, "Bobbie, I didn't think you would do it."

"I almost didn't," Bob admitted. "It was one of the toughest decisions I ever made. SAIC Buskirk called me to his office this afternoon and asked why I was leaving. I told him I was the victim of some dirty dealing during my time at ID and left it at that.

"Buskirk said he was sorry to hear that and complimented me on the 'great job' I had done at WFO. He said he didn't want to lose me and asked me to reconsider. For a couple of heartbeats, I was going to tell him that I would stay. It was a moment of truth. Then, honor and principle came to the forefront. I knew I couldn't go on working there everyday living a lie. I'm willing to confess my sin and shame at not having fought harder to change the Washington Hilton survey. But no one else is willing to admit to their mistakes or take any responsibility. I can't live in that culture. So, I told Buskirk, regretfully, that I was still leaving.

"SAIC Buskirk did tell me that I was welcome back if I ever change my mind. 'Don't think you can't come back,' he said. 'Just pick up the phone and call me.'"

"That's good news," I said. "That can be an option for you. Maybe someday you can put this all behind you and return to the Secret Service."

"Yeah, maybe," Bob replied with some hope in his voice.

Leaving the Secret Service was not something Bob wanted to do; it was something he had to do. Bob cared more about the Secret Service than he cared about his own happiness. He sacrificed his personal career for the good of the Service. He knew that if he stayed, it would only be a matter of time until he would have to make known publicly the information regarding the USSS coverup. Bob had too much integrity for his own good ... and his own peace of mind.

And as I would find out many years later, Bob felt he had failed to keep his vow to the *collective*. He should have been more persistent and taken his concerns regarding the 1978 Washington Hilton survey changes to anyone who would have listened to him at PPD.

Chapter 16

Foresight

In addition to those instances already mentioned, Bob has proven his power of foresight on many occasions through the years. One of the strangest took place when Bob was serving as a duty agent at the Secret Service's Intelligence Division.

It began one Friday evening after most everyone had left ID for the weekend. Suddenly, an Intelligence Research Specialist from the Foreign Intelligence Branch appeared at the duty desk with an anxious look on her face.

She advised Bob that ID had just received a puzzling classified teletype from a U.S. military special operations force. The teletype informed the USSS that the unit would be conducting a *surprise* test of presidential and White House security in D.C. over the weekend.

At first, Bob thought she was joking. But after assurances that the document was real and with verification at the teletype machine, the gravity of the situation set in.

Bob immediately informed the USSS Presidential Protective Division Command Post and the Uniformed Division Operations Center of the news. SAIC-ID was then notified of the situation for authority to send a reply back to the sender in no uncertain words to cancel the operation *forthwith*. Bob feared that an uncoordinated exercise might end in tragedy, as agents and officers would respond as if it were real.

Calls were also made to the National Military Command Center and the White House Military Office, which advised no knowledge of the exercise.

Later that evening, the military unit acknowledged that they had canceled the exercise. They also submitted some background on the unit with hope that the USSS would join them for future activities.

One thing caught Bob's eye. They boasted that they were the only military unit to carry their sidearms *cocked and unlocked*. This worried Bob because if the weapon was cocked with the thumb safety off, it would discharge with only a pull or bump of the trigger. To Bob, this made little sense in the nature of the unconventional operations the unit performed. A slip of the finger while approaching a target might tip off the enemy. The practice also seemed somewhat dangerous in training and combat situations where the pistol might prematurely discharge while drawing and handling, especially under heightened adrenaline. Bob conjectured that the main reason the unit carried their pistols that way was probably for *bragging rights*.

Some years later, Bob's concern became deadly reality. A member of the unit accidentally discharged his cocked and *unlocked* firearm, while he was moving behind a comrade during a live-fire training exercise. The service member struck died from his wounds.

A personally tragic example of Bob's farsightedness occurred in 1992. A neighbor's daughter was engaged to a young man with a powerful sports car. On several occasions, he dropped her off at her residence and drove in a proper manner to the corner where we lived. Then all hell broke loose! The fellow would squeal out burning rubber and fishtail down the road until disappearing at a high rate of speed. Bob caught it all from our second-floor window late one Friday night.

The next morning, Bob told me he was going to talk to the girl's father. As a former police officer, Bob saw what he described as dangerous, reckless driving. The gal was in her 20s, and we were friends of her parents. I suggested against it. I mentioned that the parents indicated to me that they really liked and thought highly of her fiancé. "She and her parents must know what's going on," I said. "The burnouts are so loud and everything. I think he's just blowing off steam on a backroad. She's a smart young lady. He can't be doing this with her in the car or to any extent."

"I have the feeling this guy drives like this more than that," replied Bob

"Please, Bobbie, let's not come off like busybody neighbors. We've already got one of those on the court. Let's give it some time."

Bob agreed to my request but said if it continues, he was going to have a heart-to-heart with the girl's dad.

Tragedy struck the *following* weekend. We arrived home; the answering machine was blinking its message light. The call was from another neighbor on the court. She related the horrific news. The couple had been coming back from Maryland's Eastern Shore. Apparently, the vehicle had been speeding excessively. The young man lost control. The vehicle went off the road into a ditch and flipped over. Both were *killed*.

Bob was grief stricken. He blamed himself for not following through with the warning to our neighbor. He felt partly responsible for the girl's death. I told him that it probably wouldn't have done any good. Her parents wouldn't have stopped her from seeing him. Bob replied, "I should have tried! They may have been able to set some rules for him when she was in the car."

Another sad event in which Bob foresaw the tragic end was the 51-day standoff in 1993 between the FBI and Branch Davidians religious sect in Waco, Texas. On April 19, 1993, Bob and I watched the end of the siege play out on live television coverage. Bob couldn't believe what was happening. The FBI was using military armored vehicles with mounted booms to punch holes into the Davidians' Mount Carmel Center.

Attached to the booms were lines leading to spray nozzles that pumped CS tear gas inside the building. After several hours with no one coming out, the ramming operation was sped up resulting in large quantities of gas going into the building. The ramming of the building eventually caused large scale structural damage. Bob watched in horror. He said many times throughout the final hours that the FBI was playing into the hands of the Davidian leader, David Koresh.

Bob had been following the siege and was familiar with Koresh and his beliefs. Bob suggested that Koresh had delusions of grandeur that manifested as divine prophecies. Koresh believed he was the second Christ, who talked directly with God.

Bob felt that the only possibility the siege would end without further bloodshed would be by long-term negotiations and waiting for the Davidians' supplies to run out. What Bob saw the FBI doing was giving an unstable Koresh confirmation that Mount Carmel was in fact Armageddon for the final battle between good and evil and the end of the world.

For weeks, the FBI had relentlessly bombarded the compound with intense light and abhorrent sound for sleep deprivation. Koresh had also been wounded earlier in the initial raid by the Bureau of Alcohol, Tobacco, and Firearms (ATF), which claimed the lives of four agents and five Davidians. It would not take much for Koresh to have ordered the fires that broke out inside the compound that day. He believed he would be reunited with his followers in the vision of the afterlife he saw. It would be the fulfillment of his delusional apocalyptic prophecy.

Bob was saddened that federal agents and our government leaders would employ such tactics against women and defenseless children and infants. "What were they thinking?" Bob declared. Although Bob believed the FBI didn't want to intentionally harm anyone, he knew their actions were a death warrant. There was nothing Bob could do but watch and wait.

The catastrophic end came at about 12 noon local time, as Bob had predicted. Fires broke out and were fanned by heavy winds. The compound was engulfed in flames. Only nine got out alive. Seventy-five bodies, which included 25-childeren, were found.

Bob admitted that it was more likely that Koresh would never have surrendered. He probably would have kept his wives, children, and true believers with him to their death and prophesied resurrection. Yet, negotiations before the final assault were successful in the release of 14 adults and 21 children. It's possible that continuing negotiations and waiting out the Davidians would have caused more to leave the compound.

"Plus, you have to worry about unintended consequences," Bob warned. "The FBI and federal government will be blamed rightly or wrongly for these deaths and 'Remember Waco' could be the rallying cry for future anti-government extremists. It would have been better if the FBI would have waited them out and taken no *aggressive* action."

Bob's worry came to a horrible fruition on the *second anniversary* of the Branch Davidian fire. On April 19, 1995, domestic terrorists Timothy McVeigh and Terry Nichols blew up the Alfred P. Murrah Federal Building in Oklahoma City, Oklahoma. One-hundred and sixty-eight souls perished including 19 children. McVeigh and Nichols cited revenge for the Waco incident as the main reason for the bombing. The Oklahoma City bombing stands alone as the worst act perpetrated by *domestic* terrorists in American history.

Chapter 17

In Conclusion

Eventually, I asked Bob some million-dollar questions. Where did he think his consciousness was before his present reincarnation? His reply, "I think the souls of the collective are nearby, but we can't see them. They may be in another dimension or only be energy particles. They can't be too far away. One moment I was in the collective, and in a flash of light I was in the hospital delivery room.

"I also think some of the UFO sightings throughout history might have been probes from other dimensions. The collective consciousness or whomever had been following Earth's history and concerned about atomic warfare. They're trying to better mankind as much as possible. They don't want our world destroyed. They're getting their information somehow.

"Think about it. Is it more probable that alien spaceships are traveling trillions of miles to reach us? Think of the many, many years it would take along with all of the necessary supplies, etc. Or are they penetrating dimensionally with more practical craft in a way that's much more feasible?

"I can add that I believe the consciousness of the universe has existed since the beginning of time. I'm pretty sure I had multiple prior lives and that I'm part of the cosmic consciousness. Believe it or not; some well-respected scientists are engaged in research to see if our awareness is part of a universal cosmic brain.

"It's possible too that some child prodigies have retained certain memory and other cognitive advances from a prior life. And why some of these fade with age. I originally remembered a lot more about the collective.

"The reason some don't have pre-birth memories and I did is probably because I was allowed to remember the vow I had made. Otherwise, I wouldn't have been able to keep it!"

As to Bob's power of foresight: Was he seeing into the future? Did he have premonitions? Bob believes he was truly allowed to keep a higher consciousness and had been gifted with exceptional cognitive abilities. These attributes enabled him to process information quickly and accurately.

"Like a computer program," Bob declared, "my mind's eye visualizes the most probable outcomes of what's been imputted. I especially see dangerous issues and how to make them safe. *I see things most people don't.* It's been a blessing and a hardship because throughout life most people saw it differently than me.

"If I made my case too hard, it turned folks off. Yet, some things I always felt so sure about. And it always seemed that my mind's eye and inner voice were right in the long run.

"I persevered in the Secret Service because I had made that vow to the collective. Otherwise, I would have used my abilities to become an attorney with an easier life and better financial rewards.

"It was sad in a way. As loyal as I was to the Service and as well as I did the job, I never got the recognition I deserved. But what bothered me the most is the Secret Service missed opportunities for their culture to grow faster and better. They didn't see what I saw. Most of my suggestions fell on death ears.

"President Reagan came *very* close to dying. Fortunately, he lived to bring down the Berlin Wall, helped to end the Cold War and fostered world peace and disarmament. All in all, I do believe that I helped to break the Presidential Curse and improved the Service, somewhat.

"It's possible that by working during the Reagan assassination attempt, I influenced the outcome of his survival. Besides actual physical actions, are some folks *consciously* able to influence outcomes? Our universe still has many things to reveal."

I comforted Bob by agreeing that his inspired efforts had bettered the USSS. Living those years with Bob and with the research I did on our book, I knew Bob had been an innovator. He was ahead of his time, especially as to behavioral analysis and PI procedures. If some top-tier Secret Service officials had listened more to Bob, the Service could have jumped many years ahead in those areas and those advances could have trickled down to other agencies and the remainder of the public and private sector. It's a tribute to Bob that today's Secret Service utilizes many of the ideas he suggested in the 70s and 80s. It's a better organization because of the changes. The USSS is the best protective agency in the world.

Next, I asked Bob what he thought was the biggest threat to American society. Bob's answer: "violence, violence, and more violence! The world is bombarded with too much violence. Not only in real life, but also on TV, in movies and video games, on the Internet, in music, books, and magazines. It's become institutionalized in our culture.

"Folks have become conditioned to it, especially youth and adolescents and those with impressionable minds and suicidal thoughts. Violence provokes copycat behavior. Some blame others for their misery. School and workplace shootings happen all too often by those who have become predisposed to violence. They angrily seek revenge and gain notoriety by perpetrating an infamous act. Too many people's and nations' first responses are violent ones! We have to find ways to get violence out of our media and our lives. Periodic anger management and de-escalation training should be mandatory in our schools and workplace."

And the final burning question: Who did Bob think killed JFK? "I'm a retired federal criminal investigator, who strongly believes in facts and evidence," Bob began. "There's overwhelming facts and evidence that Lee Harvey Oswald attempted to kill General Walker, assassinated President Kennedy, wounded Governor Connolly, and murdered Officer Tippet.

"In late September 1963, Oswald traveled to Mexico to gain entry to Cuba. He believed Marxism was alive and well in Cuba. At the Cuban Embassy, he used the ploy that he wanted to go to Russia via Cuba. He's told he must first get a visa to Russia. At the Russian Embassy, he's told it would take four months for the Soviet visa. His trip is a failure, and he returns to Dallas.

"It's possible that while in Mexico City, Cuban, Russian, or other agents conspired with Oswald. In any event, I believe it's probable that Oswald returned home desperate for his next escape from an unhappy life. Oswald got a job at the Texas School Book Depository by chance. JFK's visit to Dallas hadn't been announced yet, and the eventual motorcade route wasn't made public until a few days before the visit.

"I suggest that President Kennedy's visit to Dallas with his motorcade passing by the Texas School Book Depository was the chance of a lifetime for Oswald. A chance he couldn't pass up. He had been a committed Marxist since his teens. He considered himself a visionary and believed in Marxist revolutionary doctrine. Oswald hated capitalism, and he saw the American president as the leader of an unjust society. Destiny had given Oswald an opportunity to prove his self-perceived greatness, to further history, and *to gain entry to Cuba.*

"The JFK assassination, in my estimation, was an impulsive crime of opportunity committed by a very desperate and troubled individual. That's why Oswald had so little time to think it out and to prepare. For example, after the assassination, Oswald had to take the time to stop by his Dallas rooming house to pick up his .38-caliber revolver. If he had been set on the assassination for any great time, Oswald would already have made arrangements to have the pistol with him.

"Oswald was probably planning on *hijacking an airliner for an escape to Cuba.* That would be why he had to get the revolver from his rooming house. And why he didn't bother to pick up his passport when he was there. Oswald wouldn't need a passport to board a domestic flight and then skyjack it to Cuba or to storm his way on an airliner at gunpoint. Once in Havana, Oswald would ask for political asylum.

"But along the escape route, he's stopped by Officer Tippet. Oswald's next action showed clearly that he wasn't an innocent 'patsy' and that he didn't want to be caught. The evidence shows that Oswald mercilessly pumped four bullets into Officer Tippet—killing him instantly. Oswald's getaway to Cuba was sidetracked. He's forced to hide out in a movie theater. After he's arrested, what else could Oswald do? His only hope was to fight the charges and to win an acquittal in court.

"Unfortunately, I don't think we'll ever know for sure due to Jack Ruby silencing Oswald forever. There's one thing that continues to bother me to this day, though. Ruby used a little-known point shooting technique to kill Oswald. The method was taught to commandos in World War II. Agents of the OSS, the forerunner of the CIA, were schooled in it.

"I noticed it many years ago when I watched footage of the Oswald killing. The photographs taken at the time of the shooting confirmed it. Ruby knew what he was doing, *or* he had some very good coaching. As he sprung out of the crowd toward Oswald, Ruby extended his right arm. In his hand was a snub-nosed revolver. Unlike how most everyone else grips a handgun, Ruby had his index finger, which is the normal trigger finger, pointing along the frame of the gun in line with the barrel. He used his middle finger on the trigger. Since he wasn't using the sights, Ruby didn't need to bring the gun to eye level. This allowed him to keep the gun low and to move in quickly with stealth. This is a very effective means of accurately engaging a moving target at close quarters. Pointing his right index finger where he wanted to shoot, Ruby dispatched Oswald with one shot.

"This was never mentioned in the Warren Commission's Report. The shooting of Oswald looked more like a professional hit. I don't know where Ruby picked up the technique. He spent almost three years in the Army Air Corps, but his specialty was aircraft maintenance. Ruby didn't learn it in mechanics' school!"

Bob's concluding reflections, "The collective consciousness is pure thought and has the wisdom of the ages. It's up to all of us to make this a better world. We have *free will* and need to use it wisely. We can change our tomorrows for the better. Our future is not predetermined.

"The universe is based on the laws of physics and rules of nature. One would think if gods had unlimited powers, we'd all be healthy and happy with peace and prosperity. Since that isn't the case, those of us on Earth need to take care of ourselves and each other. We have been empowered to control our own destiny.

"In the troubled world of today, we need to work together to improve our *planet.* Instead of building more weapons of mass destruction, we should build trust and friendships with all the peoples of the world. Our leaders need to realize that we shouldn't try to *force* our culture on others, but work as friends to improve social development and to promote a universal standard of living for all. Mankind has more in common than not.

"Yes, we have to stay strong against bad actors, while reaching out to find ways in which we can resolve our problems peaceably. We should treat those less fortunate with dignity and be willing to help them. We share a special place in the universe, and we must always remember to be grateful and to cherish the life we have been given. Don't take it for granted!

"At home and around the world, we should commit to clean up the land, skies, and oceans—using more of our resources in peaceful ways that better mankind. Every day should be Earth Day.

"Whatever your beliefs are as to an afterlife, we are here and can make a difference *now*. Do right and be happy! Act in positive ways, have a clean conscience, and be remembered for the betterment, love, and joy you brought to our world. Believe me, you *will* be held accountable for your actions.

"I know from experience that one's soul, spirit, consciousness, or whatever you wish to call it survives the death of the human body and carries on. With pandemics, terrorists, mass murders, war, everyday violence, and the like, this message needs to get out. I hope it will comfort those who have lost friends and loved ones.

"Our true book provides some *rational* explanation to issues of faith and spirituality. Hopefully, it will inspire others to offer any pre-birth recollections they may have."

PROLOGUE

We hope you enjoyed our story. Now, it's up to you. Think back to your earliest memories. Did *you* choose your parents? Do you have any pre-birth stories or similar events to tell? If so, we look forward to reading them soon.

With your support, this phenomenon can be studied by scientists and philosophers. ...

OUR NEW BEGINNING

ABOUT THE AUTHORS

J an Marie and Bob Ritter live on the shores of the Chesa-
peake Bay in Southern Maryland. Both are graduates of the
University of Maryland and longtime residents of the
Washington Metropolitan Area.

Jan Marie is retired from the teaching profession where she
specialized in Early Childhood Education and Reading Recovery. When not walking the boardwalk for exercise, she enjoys
shopping, antiquing, reading and working crossword puzzles.

Bob is a retired federal criminal investigator (GS-1811) with a
wealth of law enforcement and protective experience. A born
collector, Bob loves history and the music of the 1940s–60s. He
takes pleasure in watching the wildlife and ships that pass by
the couple's Bay-front condominium. Bob is a member of the
U.S. Secret Service Association, the Federal Law Enforcement
Officers Association, the Fraternal Order of Police, and the National Law Enforcement Museum.

Jan Marie and Bob relish spending time with family and
friends, especially the couple's five granddaughters. They
deeply love one another and cherish each day together.

Did You Choose Your Parents? is the remarkable story of
Bob's dedication to making our world a better place.

Jan Marie and Bob Ritter

In the Secret Service Years